MYTHS
OF
EDUCATION

TRUTHS that will Set You Free

Margie Abbitt

DEDICATION

To God who has led me through this journey of discovering many truths about education.

To my husband, Mac, who supported me every step of the way.

Blessings to more people than I can count who I learned from in one way or another, especially my children.

Blessings to the many people who lent a helping hand to make this book possible.

TABLE OF CONTENTS

INTRODUCTION

I don't consider myself a writer! I DO, however, consider myself a storyteller. I feel like I have a story to tell about my education journey and what I have learned over the decades that will help parents make wise decisions about their children's education.

In the first section of this book, I will tell you some of "**My Story**" that laid a platform for me to learn about education. In the next section of the book, I will present one **MYTH** at a time with what I believe to be the **TRUTH.** Then I will discuss what I have discovered and share my experiences and my stories for you to ponder. Hopefully, learning these **TRUTHS** will empower you to be set free from a traditional school mindset so that you and your child are set free to get a great education. These **MYTHS** come from actual conversations with thousands of parents over the years. You may find that I present a myth and truth in more than one way because parents ask the questions in different ways, and sometimes accepting the change to this new way of thinking about education needs more than one application to be understood.

Throughout this book you will find some **Funny NOW Stories**. I call them this because I like to find humor in the crazy things of life. Many of these stories were not funny when they happened, and I might have had to remind myself and my family that the momentary affliction would be a memory one day. However, with time and enough distance from those events, I have a different perspective now. I hope that you will find the humor in some of my stories and find yourself laughing along as well. In other stories, I hope what I share will encourage you that you are not alone in your education journey and your experiences.

I do mention throughout the book my stories about co-ops. I realized early on that working together with other families to educate our children was extremely beneficial. We called these groups "co-ops" because parents were cooperating with each other to educate our children.

As you continue to read through this book, I hope you will pick up nuggets of education gold that will enrich your journey. I call them "nuggets of gold" because that is what each lesson I learned was worth to me. I also hope you will read it again later and grasp other gold pieces to sustain you during other steps on your path. And, I hope your eyes are opened to other golden **TRUTHS** that I may not have mentioned.

There were many things that I believed because of

my traditional education experience. Eventually, I realized they were just **MYTHS** and many times the opposite was where the truth would be found.

- One definition of a myth is "a folklore genre consisting of narratives that play a fundamental role in a society."

Traditional schools, both public and private, have played a fundamental role in our society. In my reading about the establishment of the public school system in America, one controversy that stands out is the purpose of public education. It was to train students to become skilled workers while teaching them the traditional academic disciplines. The terms "factory model school" and "industrial era schools" emerged. A great resource on this subject is *The Underground History of American Education* by John Taylor Gatto.

I first heard about the "factory model school" when I took an Educational Psychology class in college in 1991. It is debated that the elite of America wanted to train factory workers for their industries who would be used to responding to a whistle blowing or a bell ringing. However, one might believe traditional academic disciplines would only include reading, writing, and arithmetic–subjects most parents would gladly accept help in teaching. Unfortunately, the major concern is that the education system has gone far beyond these topics and has become a system where students are taught what to think and not to think for themselves.

Consider a system where students are given a book, told to read it, memorize the concepts and then prove mastery of those concepts on a test. If you can make the coveted "A" on the test then you are dubbed "SMART." If you can't, then you are not smart. I hear parents all the time refer to the child that makes A's as smart and one who doesn't as not so smart.

The concern continues to grow that people are easier to control and manipulate if they are not allowed to be free thinkers and develop their own ideas. A Free Thinker like Thomas Edison was sent home from his traditional school and labeled as useless because he did not fit in with the traditional way of doing things. History proved he was a genius.

As we journey through this book together and discuss the myths, I pray that you will pick up each nugget of **TRUTH** and put it in your education bucket. I hope these **TRUTHS** pave the path to a rewarding and smoother journey educating according to your children's gifts.

For the most part this is a book of my opinions and

observations of education for over half a century. You may not agree with everything I share, but I hope, at the very least, the ideas presented in this book will make you more observant of what is happening in the world of education so you can choose what is best for your children.

I realized in the very early parts of my journey that I had a "public school trained brain." However, throughout my journey, God took me from being chained in a cage of ideas of what school **should** look like to being set free to educate my children according to the way they learned best.

So, Brace Yourself
as you get ready to encounter truths
that will set you free to homeschool.

MY STORY

Since the 1990s, I have been doing workshops to help people understand what true education should look like. One of my favorite workshops is called *Set Free to Homeschool; It's Not Traditional School*. In it, I share things I wished I had known when I started homeschooling. This workshop is the basis for the book that you now hold in your hands. I am super excited to share with you my story and experiences on this journey. Let's get started!

My fascination with education did not begin when we started homeschooling our children. Rather, it was when I was in the 3rd grade, and I would tutor the neighborhood kids on the back porch at my parents' house. Students that struggled to learn math in school were learning from a 3rd grader. I realized at a young age that students learned better with one-on-one attention, and when learning was fun as well. "Playing School" with neighbor kids was so much fun for me. When the parents realized that their children's math skills were improving, they encouraged my mom to let me "play school" the next summer too.

Even though I had a very traditional school experience with teachers lecturing, doing worksheets, and taking tests, I learned best if I could hear what I needed to know. I would go into my bedroom and read my schoolwork out loud so I could remember what I was reading. My siblings thought this was so silly, but for me it was a game changer for being successful at school.

As a child I had a lazy eye. Later on I came to realize that I also have some characteristics of dyslexia, as well. I think these challenges gave me a heart of compassion for people who don't learn like others.

Another part of my story that built my compassion for people who are different is that I am color-blind. I was told when I was young that only about one in every million girls is colorblind. It wasn't easy being this special. It creates many challenges even today. But my mom was great at helping me adapt since my father was color-blind, and so was my mom's father. She had been around it all her life and she taught me from a young age several techniques to deal with life situations, like memorizing what color things should be. This worked great, except that I was an adult before I knew grass wasn't necessarily green in the wintertime.

Funny NOW Story: When I was in 5th grade, the class was given an assignment to look at a colored map with different shades of brown and green to show the topography like mountains, plateaus, valleys, etc. The teacher wanted us to look at the book and color a map in class. I quickly realized I would need help and went to the teacher. When I told him that I was color-blind, he accused me of lying because girls are not color-blind. He decided that I needed to be paddled for lying. Yes, corporal punishment was a thing when I was in school. I knew I did not lie, and all I knew to do was to take off running. When I got to the office, they called my mom. But it was my color-blind dad who left work and showed up at school. He could not believe that it had never been put in my school records and that I could have been punished for being color-blind. Maybe this is one reason my dad was my hero. I knew then it was important for parents to be involved and I knew what it was like for teachers to not understand my challenge in education.

My dad had his own story about his experience with school which made an impression on me as a child. My dad was very smart. He could build or fix anything he set his mind to. I believe this impacted my view of where education happens. I will tell you more of his story later.

Funny NOW Story: Another experience that I learned from happened in 8th grade. My twin brother and I had done very well in the county school we attended for elementary school, but for junior high we moved closer to the city where we were enrolled in the 7th grade. There was a class for "accelerated students", but we were not allowed to be in that class because we came from the county school. This worked okay for 7th grade, but when we got to 8th grade and students were randomly placed in class together, I ended up in a class where all but three students were struggling learners.

The first day of math class the teacher had the students write their numbers 1 to 100. I could do long division in my head. The teacher quickly realized I was bored, so I was sent to the library where I would spend hours in a self-study program to keep me busy. I was so bored that my mom decided to request they make an exception and put me in the accelerated class. I thought this would be a good thing, but I quickly realized most of the students were accelerated in cheating. I didn't want any part of it. And then the bullying began.

There was this one girl who would make sure she sat next to me in the library, and when no one was looking she would punch me in the arm over and over. I am not sure why I put up with the bullying, but I would pray that God would take her away. After Christmas break, her family moved to another city. I got to see the hand of God answer my prayer. I also learned that putting a lot of pressure on students to succeed can drive them to do whatever it takes to make good grades, even cheat and bully others.

In high school I really loved helping other students learn math and thought I would go to college to be a math teacher. But before my senior year, the guidance counselor suggested I take accounting as my senior math. Then, next thing I knew, I was applying to go to a business college to study accounting. This wasn't all bad because I met my husband at my first job out of college. The humorous thing is that he got an accounting degree because he didn't want to be a teacher like his parents.

Since my background was steeped in traditional education and accounting, it might lead you to think that I was not very creative, but very analytical. Like most accountants, I liked sticking to standards and rules. One of God's first miracles with us was getting two cost accountants to commit their lives to Christ. Another miracle was to convince them to homeschool their children, which was basically unheard of and very out of the box in the 1980s.

In addition, my husband's parents were in public school education where his father was a principal/teacher, and his mom was a biology teacher. Both were well

17

educated and believed highly in the public education system. Neither of our families encouraged our decision to homeschool, but we just knew homeschool was what God wanted us to do. Some family members said nothing to our faces. But others were very outspoken and even divisive in their objection to our decision. Amazingly, our conviction never wavered that homeschooling was our path to take. We took it one year at a time, asking God to show us if it was His will for us to continue homeschooling. When I would get discouraged, God always sent hope and confirmation.

Despite the adversity, we would not have traded the opportunity we had to home educate our children for anything, but we did learn a lot through that journey. Our journey in homeschooling started in the 1980s when our first child was born. While that was decades ago, it doesn't feel like it has been that long because we have had an incredible journey.

The Lord blessed us with six children. Let me explain what this looked like. There is a fourteen-year age span between the oldest child and the youngest. My oldest child was in high school when I had my last baby. Our three boys are each spaced about seven years apart with three girls sprinkled in between the boys. This completed our "Brady Bunch" family. All in all, it took about thirty years to complete the homeschool journey.

Each one of our children had different personalities, learning styles, attitudes, gifts and talents, etc. We wondered how these children could have come from the same two parents. You will hear more about them throughout this book. Here is a little synopsis:

Everything came easier for Child 1, our first-born son. By the time I thought to teach him something as simple as how to put on his coat when he was two, he was already doing it from watching someone else. I would keep toys in neat little baskets, and he would play with one toy at a time. I thought that parenting wasn't going to be that hard.

Then Child 2, a girl, was born and brought a whole different dynamic to our family which I was not expecting. After she was born and they gave her to me, she stuck her long tongue out at me, and I didn't know that was a prophetic warning. From day one, she would learn when and how she wanted to. She loved to take my neat little baskets and dump them all in the middle of the floor to play. We practiced a lot of sorting skills as we put things back in order.

I felt like God waited five years to give me Child 3, another son, so that there would be four of us to keep him safe. We called him the "Energizer Bunny." My mom commented when visiting that he never had the same thing in his hands twice, which earned him another nickname–the "Little Tornado." We thought it would be great if we could slow him down enough to teach him to read by the time he was nine.

Then God gave us the "Calm After the Storm" with our sweet Child 4, another girl. She was the quiet observer who learned from the others' mistakes. She liked things to be neat and orderly. If someone spilled a little water on the table, she would stop eating until it was cleaned up. She struggled a little bit with the pronunciation of words, but she is an overcomer in every challenge of life.

Next, I had a baby that left my womb too soon. We named him Gabriel because he was going to live with the angels. My mom gave me a song called, "Jesus has a Rocking Chair" that helped me through this painful time. I share this part of my story because I don't want to give the impression in any way that there wasn't heartache along the journey, but God reassured me of His faithfulness no matter what.

I didn't want my motherhood journey to end that way. So a year later, God gave us Child 5, who had to be one of the most loving children one could meet. If you met her today, she would want to give you a hug. From a very young age, she loved to draw and loved animals. She was kind of an animal and children "whisperer" as she got older. However, in her young years, we realized that learning reading, writing, and math did not come naturally to her. Her love and determination took her much further than we ever imagined, and I probably learned the most about education from watching what it took for her to learn.

Then we became "The Parents of the Last Child." We had been warned not to become lax with the last child, so we tried our best, but his personality was like none of the rest. I had another homeschool mom give me a book called the *Two Sides of Love* by Gary Smalley and John Trent that compared personalities to a lion, a beaver, a golden retriever, and an otter. She warned me that I might question my sanity if I didn't understand that the wonderful free-spirited last Child 6 had the personality of an otter. Child 6 was in his own world. One of us constantly had to have an eye on him or we would lose him, which we did several times. If you have ever seen an otter at the zoo just jumping in and out of the water without a care in the world, that was Child 6. If you tried to discipline him, it didn't seem to faze him. He would immediately start talking about something else he was interested in, like maybe a squirrel outside. This child was my biggest challenge.

For more about the zoo at my house, check out
my webinar *How Children Learn Best.*

The differences between all my children really kept me on my toes, or maybe I should say knees, trying to figure out what was going to open each child's eyes to education. We did not do everything right; we made a lot of mistakes. And if it was possible to go back and do it over, I would change some things based on what I learned along the way... especially with my two older children. God bless all of them for having endured many times when we didn't have a clue what we were doing. I often think that God gave me two children, waited five years, and then said, "*Try again.*" And then He gave us four more children.

One day after my children were grown, I was just talking to the Lord. I told Him I wanted to have a "do over" because I had learned so much over the last 30 years. What He spoke to my heart was that every time I help another parent, it's my "do over." In other words, when I take what I have learned and pass it forward, it is like seeing my do over in other families' lives. So, what I really hope I get to do as you read this book is just give you a different perspective to what education can look like and how you can enjoy the journey of education as a lifestyle with your children.

CHAPTER 1

Myths About Parent's Responsibilities for Their Children's Education

Myth 1: *Education is too complicated for parents. It takes people with degrees to educate.*

TRUTH : Education is not and does not have to be complicated. Parents become teachers at the birth of their first child. You do not need a college degree to educate your children.

Homeschooling in the 1980s was not "normal." When we mentioned to our families that we were going to homeschool, we received a much less than warm response. Even my very sweet mother-in-law, who was a biology teacher, asked, "What makes you think you can teach a child to read?" I guess I would have felt more intimidated at the time if our four-and-a-half-year-old oldest son wasn't already reading. Even though I was just a mom, I had managed to teach him to eat, walk, talk, know his colors, numbers, letters, and he was even reading. Note: All my children absolutely did not read this early.

One of my family members was very vocal about her objections to our decision, but she would talk about how much time she spent with her daughter doing homework after being at school all day. I realized she was really homeschooling at night, and I was homeschooling in the morning during the best hours of my child's day. Of course, with my traditional school mindset, I still thought that education began at five years old when a child starts "real" school, and that "real" teachers had to have a college degree on the wall for students to get a "real" education. I thought I wasn't a "real" teacher because I did not have a teaching certificate. Maybe you feel the same way.

Some of the first curriculum that was available to homeschoolers was traditional school curriculum. Our first reading workbook came with a teacher's guide that told the teacher exactly what to say to the student and how the student should respond. I remember thinking that this kind of guide made it easy for "real" teachers to teach.

Even with the revelation about the teacher's guide, as I was educating my children at home, it still took me about seven years to realize **I am a teacher.** I realized that I had been their teacher from birth. Even though there were things I had never been taught or couldn't remember being taught, I discovered I could learn along with my children. As we learned together, it dawned on me that I was developing my own love for learning and redeeming my own education by learning with my children.

A very wise man said to me recently to think back over my education experience and recall which teachers had made the biggest difference in my life. Then he asked if those teachers had a master's degree or a doctorate degree. I did not know, nor did I care about their educational background. I just remembered that they cared about me and I learned in their classes. Then I remembered that my grandfather, who taught school, went to school when there were only eight grades. He received a diploma in the eighth grade and taught school with only an 8th grade diploma.

Parents are generally the best people to oversee and make decisions about their children's education because no one else is typically going to care more about their child's education than the parents. A parent's love motivates them to keep learning and finding the best ways to educate their children. Having a college degree doesn't guarantee a better education. This doesn't mean parents won't use other teachers, resources, schools, etc. to be a part of their plan. But parents need to be the ones deciding what is best for their children.

****

Myth 2: *Parents can't possibly know enough to teach their children.*

TRUTH: Parents can learn along with their children and will redeem their own education while their children are learning.

You don't need to be concerned that you are not smart enough or don't know enough or didn't do well enough in school. Guide your student into learning and you can learn along with them. Who knows, they may end up knowing more than you, and that is okay.

What you need to teach your children is basic:
1. A Love of Learning
2. A Good Work Ethic
3. Problem Solving Skills

The "schoolly" kinds of things your children really need to know are READING, WRITING, and ARITHMETIC.

My parents and grandparents knew this was the basis of a good education. For the many generations that came before them, this was all that was required to be considered "educated." Most parents in America can read, write, and do basic math.   And therefore, parents are qualified to share this knowledge with their children. Parents can learn everything else alongside their children.

Funny NOW Story: When I ordered my curriculum for kindergarten, I chose CLASS (Christian Liberty Academy of Satellite Schools) because it seemed the friendliest toward the idea of homeschooling. When the box arrived, reality hit that we were going to teach our children at home: *I was responsible for my son's education.* I began to cry inconsolably over the top of the box. My tears were literally making the top of the box wet, and my hands shook as I prayed for help. *What was I doing?* Then the verse "I can do all things through Christ who strengthens me" came to my mind. I thought surely God could give me the strength to open the box. When I opened the box there was a letter on top, and I will never forget how the letter started. It said, "You may feel overwhelmed right now, but remember: you can do all things through Christ who strengthens you." I knew God was with me and had given me confirmation to move forward.

That box contained numerous workbooks, including a phonics book and a teacher's guide for each lesson. It gave step by step instructions on what to ask the student and what the student's appropriate response should be. This is standard for teacher's editions. As I used these guides, I thought anybody could teach with these step-by-step guidelines. And before long, I did not need the guidelines anymore. It was just common sense. As a parent you know a lot more than you think.

REMEMBER: God is with you and will provide what you need. Keep it simple.

Younger ones in K-2nd grade will typically be working on phonics, reading skills, and basic math. In the process of learning to read or do math, not every student is an overnight success. And in the end, no one would care if your student learned to read at age three or age nine.

Language Arts in 3rd – 8th Grade curriculum may include grammar, spelling, reading, comprehension, poetry, and literature–which are all Language Arts topics. The beauty of home educating your student is that you can work on what they need to know and skip what they already know in the curriculum.

Myth 3: *Parents need to have all the answers.*

TRUTH: Parents don't need to know everything. They guide their children in how to find the answers and build a love for learning.

Our children amazed us with their 'why' questions like "why does that thing work that way?" It could feel intimidating and even humbling to not know the answers. We discovered **THE WORLD IS OUR CLASSROOM!**

Together we would explore our world to find the answers whether through research, experiments, or reading books. When my children were young and they asked a 'why' question, I would say, "Let's go find a book and learn that together." As they got older, I was able to say, "That's a great question. I would love to know that, too. Why don't you find out and let me know the answer?" I have never met a teenager that didn't love to tell their parents something their parents didn't know. Many times, my lack of knowledge was great motivation for my children to go find the answer. They would come back a week or two later and tell us all they had learned.

The beautiful thing is that when a child narrates or tells back what they have learned, this builds up retention of information. Statistics show that there is a 90% chance children will never forget what they discover if they verbally tell someone what he/she has learned. I also realized that my love for learning was increasing right along with my children.

One fascinating discovery of our homeschool journey was that when our kids finished high school and went off to college or went off to do whatever they wanted to do, they did very well at researching anything they needed to know. They had learned how to find information and solve problems.

People who solve problems, instead of just giving up, generally have a good attitude as they look for solutions. People who can problem solve are not going to sit down and say, "Oh, pitiful me, I just don't know how to do that." Our children had learned to get in the game and try to find an answer. Children who can solve problems learn to ask for information, not only from a book, but also, from many wise people around them. So, in home education, every day is a school day! **THE WORLD IS OUR CLASSROOM!** We learn with our students!

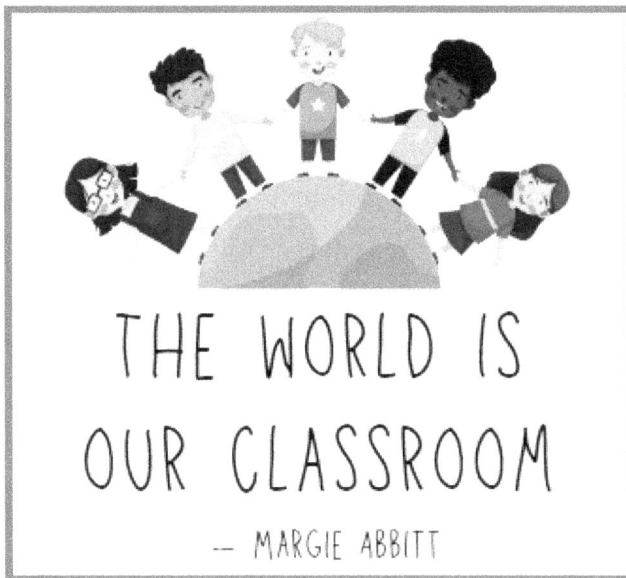

THE WORLD IS OUR CLASSROOM

-- MARGIE ABBITT

Funny NOW Story: One time I remember guiding my son into finding answers was at a homeschool event where I had a booth and was scheduled for workshops. My son was a great help in getting our old station wagon unloaded while I set up the booth. Just as I finished and headed to my first workshop, he walked up to me obviously distraught. He informed me that he had locked my keys in the car. I told him that he had a whole hour while I was speaking to figure out how to get my keys out. Then I pointed to an older gentleman in the exhibit hall and suggested that my son talk to him about the situation. An hour later when I came back to the booth, my son proudly presented me with the keys. He told me how the gentleman showed him how to use a coat hanger to unlock the car door. He solved the problem and added to his life skills.

Our children were learning much more than I had learned from my education. Even though I was learning a lot right along with them, many times they would amaze me with the facts and knowledge they were picking up and understanding.

Funny NOW Story: Our oldest son had a way of saying things factually without really processing how it would sound to others, or maybe he did it just to get a rise out of me. One day, he very matter-of-factly said, "Mom, I think I am smarter than you." Oh, only by the grace of God could I have a kind response. I pondered what he had said for a minute and replied, "Son, I hope you are. I am working hard to teach you all I know, and I hope you learn much more. However, I will always be twenty-three years wiser than you. Wisdom is gained through time, experience and trusting God, and you will never catch up with me." I was twenty-three years old when he was born and therefore twenty-three years wiser than him.

REMEMBER: Wisdom will always be your advantage.

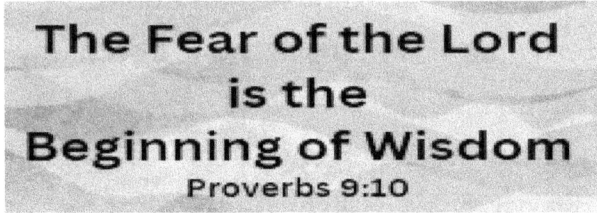

> ## The Fear of the Lord
> ## is the
> ## Beginning of Wisdom
> ### Proverbs 9:10

Myth 4: *I only feel comfortable with traditional school methods. I don't think I can change. I'm just not creative enough to think any other way.*

TRUTH: **Anyone can change and adopt and adapt to learning methods that will give their child the unique learning experience they need.**

When I hear parents say that they are not as creative as I seem to be, it makes me laugh. In the beginning, I was so caged in by the traditional school mindset. I wanted everything to be neat, timely, and orderly. I had a school schedule which only worked with the first child. My creativity, flexibility, and willingness to try new approaches to learning grew over time.

Funny NOW Stories: When our son got a bucket of Duplo blocks and wanted to pour them in a different bucket, I can remember saying that he needed to play with them using the bucket that they came in because they didn't belong in the other bucket. Looking back at my response, I want to say to myself, "Are you kidding?" I was on a path to stifling his creativity. With God's help I was able to see that my son's way of playing was a form of creativity and something to be embraced and encouraged.

When I realized that doing the same thing as traditional school was not going to give my children the best education, I was willing to change and allow the chains surrounding the cage of our home learning experience to loosen and fall off. If God could change this traditional, perfectionistic, analytical cost accountant into a creative, flexible homeschool mom, He can surely help you to be set free to homeschool. I knew that if I wanted to experience something different for my children's education, I would have to be a different kind of educator. I didn't know that our journey would be even more radical than the concept of homeschooling in the 1980s. We figured out real fast that homeschooling like everyone else, who used only textbooks and workbooks, was not going to work for our family to achieve the best education experience for us.

Myth 5: *We need the Internet in order to homeschool.*

TRUTH: Even though a lot of good resources can be found on the Internet, you do not need the Internet to educate.

During the early years of homeschooling, most homes had no computers, and the Internet wasn't even a thing. Yes, people homeschooled without the Internet. Almost every homeschooler I knew was using a private school curriculum, which was a lot of textbooks, workbooks, worksheets, quizzes, tests, and lectures about each subject. I was replicating a traditional school at home, but I didn't need a computer and at that time, neither did traditional schools.

After two years of trying the "read a book and take a test method," I realized I had to clear the chalkboard of my public-school trained brain. Each step of the way God erased from my brain traditional ideas in order to find out how education really works, what education really looks like, and when education happens.

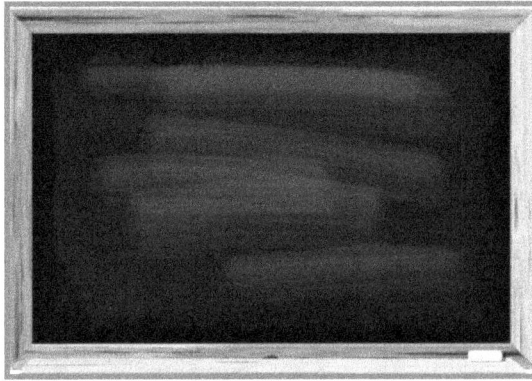

We had to go back to the basics, so much so that we named our homeschool "Back-To-Basics Academy." I loved the old song "Basics of Life" by 4Him. The chorus is:

> *We need to get back to the basics of life*
> *A heart that is pure and a love that is blind*
> *A faith that is fervently grounded in Christ*
> *The hope that endures for all times*
> *These are the basics*
> *We need to get back to the basics of life*

Sometimes the basics are the simple things: reading, writing, arithmetic, relationship building, and loving to learn.

Instead of computers and the Internet, we used a lot of library books, which were free if we returned them on time. Encyclopedias and dictionaries were common resources in most homes. We read about topics that we planned to go out and experience. When we had experiences that sparked our curiosity, we would go find a book to learn more. Our children developed a love for learning and in the process they discovered how they learned best. Through these kinds of educational experiences, each child's gifts and talents emerged.

Funny NOW Story: Not only was the Internet not available when we started homeschooling, neither were VHS tapes.

I remember the first time a mom brought an educational VHS tape to a co-op day. All the rest of us wondered if this was a legitimate way to educate our kids. Before this day, we thought education had to be reading books and taking tests. We had difficulty realizing this was an acceptable way to share knowledge. Many of us parents had never had access to audio visual aids like VHS tapes. When we were in school ourselves, there may have been an occasional reel to reel projector presentation.

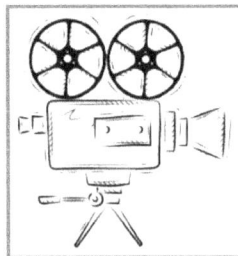

Guideline for the Internet:

When using the Internet, take a Philippians 4:8 approach: believers are encouraged to think about everything that is true, noble, lovely, admirable, excellent and praiseworthy. If you apply these principles to the Internet and its use, it will be a great guideline for what you allow your children to be exposed to on the Internet. Here's a great resource:

https://www.parentswhofight.com/

I am not saying the Internet is bad or can't be used; just don't make it your only source of learning. In addition, be aware that too much screen time can inhibit education and creativity. It has been researched for years that the rapid movement in TV programs and video games can hinder reading. Like any tool it needs to be used with great care and supervision.

REMEMBER: Many intelligent and brilliant people lived, invented, explored, and produced great things long before the Internet.

Myth 6: *How will I teach my child everything they need to know?*

TRUTH: You will never teach your children everything, but if you teach them to love to learn, they will learn for the rest of their life.

I know this is a question, not a statement, but it is a question I hear very often from many parents. It is based on a myth that we can somehow teach our children everything they will need to know. My response to that question has become, "Did your traditional education teach you everything you needed to know before you got out of school?" The answer is nearly always preceded by a chuckle and then "No!" or "Absolutely Not!"

I would personally say that ninety percent of what I know, I've learned while home educating my children. My public-school education consisted of reading textbooks, listening to lectures, taking tests and having those test scores averaged to determine how smart they perceived me to be. Even though I was pretty good at getting A's, that did not mean I really "learned" or retained the information I read or was taught long term.

A love for learning is what keeps people learning the rest of their lives. I realized when I saw the light bulbs come on in my children's eyes, they were developing a love for learning. Each time we did an experiment and their eyes lit up with the joy of discovery, each time we went on a field trip and they made a connection, I could see the excitement in their eyes. I became addicted to seeing them get excited about learning and figuring things out for themselves. I would never teach them everything they would need to know for life, but I could empower them with a love for learning and the ability to discover what they would need to learn in the future. This revelation was what really brought me to understand that no one will ever teach a child everything they will need to know. But *if you teach them to love to learn, they will learn for the rest of their lives*. And that is one of the most valuable things your children can walk away with into adulthood.

Ask yourself, "Is the way I am teaching my children getting them excited about learning? Are my children developing a love for learning or am I just reading and checking off workbook pages to feel a sense of accomplishment? Do my children get up in the morning asking, 'What else can I learn?'"

My children have gone on to learn things I would never have thought to teach them and would never have been covered in any standard curriculum. They love the opportunity to learn new things. One of our boys said that the one thing all our children have in common is that they are "learning junkies." They have different interests, but they don't hesitate to jump in and learn new things which comes from their love for learning.

Myth 7: *Homeschooling means I don't have to get out of my comfort zone.*

TRUTH: You need to get out of your comfort zone to bring enjoyment to your home education journey.

Many times, home educating successfully means we stop doing what is familiar and what makes us comfortable. The decision to homeschool, for most people, is a big jump out of what feels known and familiar and into unfamiliar territory. You may have thought you would never be one of those strange people who doesn't let their kids go to "regular" school. Many parents try everything to avoid homeschooling. I have heard people, including myself, say "I could never homeschool my children. I am not organized enough, patient enough, smart enough..." only to come back around to start homeschooling.

To be the most successful at homeschool, you don't need to replicate traditional school at home. I encourage you to leave what is known and familiar so you can enter a *Learning Zone*. We all like to stay in our comfort zone, but a Learning Zone is where the magic happens. It's where you see your kids get excited and connect their environment with what they are learning. And it is where you begin to figure out how each of your children learns best. I would even propose that gifts and strengths will come to the surface that you didn't know existed.

Funny NOW Story: One time at a convention, a mom came to talk to me with a high school planning sheet all filled out. She had Spanish listed for every year of high school. This meant she planned for her student to take a foreign language all four years of high school - which is fine. However, when I said, "Wow, your student must really love foreign language?" She said, "No, not really. I do." And I said, "I thought this was your student's education plan," and I saw the light bulb go on in her head. This mom felt comfortable teaching foreign languages because it interested her. My children have led me into areas I knew nothing about, and I had to depend on God for his provision.

Funny NOW Story: I am the opposite of the mom above. I have no interest in foreign languages. I learned nothing in my Spanish classes in high school, but I had a daughter that wanted to learn Latin. I didn't know why this was her heart's desire. Her father had taken Greek and Hebrew in seminary, but she wanted Latin. I had no desire to learn Latin. However, I wanted to help her; so, we prayed. Note: At this time in homeschooling, parents did all the teaching unless we were in co-ops. To our amazement, I was contacted by a mom about homeschooling who was the Latin professor at a local university. (I didn't even know the local university offered Latin.) In our conversation, she asked if I thought the homeschoolers would want to attend a Latin class if she offered it at her home. I immediately said, "Sign my daughter up as your first student."

As parents, we want what is best for our children. It is important that we are focused on our children's goals and not try to put our own goals and dreams in them. Moving out of your comfort zone gives you the chance to do some things you may have never done or thought about before.

People have said to me that they are not good at doing field trips. I had never planned a field trip until I started homeschooling, but if it meant my children would get a better education, I was willing to forfeit some of my comfort and make phone calls to plan field trips. After a few years, I was nicknamed the "Field Trip Queen" because I had planned so many field trips and made them available to other homeschooling families.

Just making the decision to homeschool gets people started out of their comfort zone. Getting out of my comfort zone was not easy and I was stretched regularly. However, as I saw the results, I became more comfortable, and I would not trade it for anything. I encourage you to take that next step. There is a lot of freedom when you get out of your comfort zone.

Myth 8: *Excuses justify staying in my comfort zone.*

TRUTH: To help your child learn and grow you have to let go of excuses; embrace new learning opportunities for yourself as you set the example.

Some of the excuses that I hear for not doing something different are:
- It takes too much time to teach that way.
- I am not creative enough to teach that way.
- I do not learn that way.

- It is easier to just use workbooks or a computer program.
- I work a full-time or part-time job.

Finding a way to overcome these excuses, and anything else that comes up, is worth the time you will invest. Being clear about your expectations for your child's education, whether educating at home or choosing a traditional public or private school, is worth the time.

My husband says, "Work smarter, not harder." When you educate your children at home, you will gain freedom and flexibility that traditional education choices cannot offer. Here are some ideas, suggestions, and resources to help you get out of your comfort zone:

1. **Connect with other homeschoolers** and share the responsibilities of planning activities. I do a whole workshop called <u>Working Together Works</u> where I share things I learned from teaching in co-ops and tutorials for about twenty-five years. Most of those years I was the one who started and organized opportunities for homeschool families to work together.

2. **I learned from other homeschool moms** many of the creative things I know. Usually, these creative parents needed an organizer mom. As each family shared their resources and talents, we accomplished a whole lot more than we could have accomplished alone. Today there are new groups sprouting up

every year and you can join one already established or start your own to fit your needs.

3. **I learned how to work efficiently** to get three nourishing meals on the table a day. I had to keep up with the massive amount of laundry for a family of eight people. And I wanted a clean home. Check out the How to Survive Homeschooling workshop on YouTube where we share a lot of ideas that may help you.

4. **Get help from your children**. You are preparing your children to be adults. Teach them early to be a part of taking care of the home. Even little ones can empty small trash cans into big ones or fold clothes. My little ones loved to hold the dustpan when I would sweep. If they are busy helping you, they will not be somewhere making another mess. Older children should be learning how to cook, clean the bathroom, sweep and vacuum the floors, wash dishes, do laundry, mow the grass, etc. All these things prepare them to be adults, and it also takes some of the load off the parents. Your children live in your house. Part of homeschooling is teaching them to take care of a home.

5. **Get help from friends and neighbors.** We could not afford to hire help. But with six children and my husband wearing many hats as a seminary student, pastor, and a self-employed contractor, God knew I

needed help and He brought beautiful, retired people into our lives.

We had a sweet neighbor, Eleanor, who asked me one day what she could do to help. I told her it would mean a lot to me if my children's socks were matched. She would come over once a week and sit on the couch matching socks. Our children would read her books and visit with her while she worked. I learned that Eleanor had seven children of her own and knew how busy a mother is even without homeschooling. When she passed away, all my children felt like they had lost an adopted grandmother. I'm not sure who was the most blessed. I bet you have people around you that would love to give you a hand.

Our children's grandparents lived out of state; so, we adopted a gentleman from our church as Grandpa Joe. There are no words to explain how much we all love Grandpa Joe. His unconditional love for our children was amazing. Our youngest daughter struggled with reading, and no one knew much at all back then about dyslexia and other learning challenges. Grandpa Joe would come over two or three times a week and patiently sit and help our precious daughter try to learn to read. The extra attention in a busy family meant so much to her.

Grandpa Joe had an impact on my other

children too. He would play games and ask them how they thought things worked. He always made sure they had bikes to ride and took them on neighborhood bike rides to give me a little peace and quiet. This retired engineering professor taught me so much about asking questions to promote learning rather than always giving the answer. Grandpa Joe was a blessing to us all and, I believe, he was blessed as well. Look around and see if you have an "Eleanor" or a "Grandpa Joe." They may be waiting to be asked.

6. **If you have more than one child, use the "Teach to the Oldest Child" method.** If I had all six children, each on a different science curriculum, I could not have handled it. With the "Teach to the Oldest Child" approach, the older ones would be interacting and learning with the younger ones. If I was teaching biology to the oldest child and he was studying plants, everybody else was going to be studying plants. We did field trips together on whatever we were studying. When the older children explained what they learned and the younger children were listening, it increased everyone's retention of information, including momma.

Remember: Here's a saying that sums this up:

A COMFORT ZONE IS
A BEAUTIFUL PLACE,
BUT NOTHING EVER
GROWS THERE.

Myth 9: *Because I was never good at a certain subject (math, science, writing papers, etc.) I could never teach that subject to my children.*

TRUTH: GOOD TEACHERS NEVER STOP LEARNING.
Learning never stops for anyone. You don't have to know everything in order to teach your children.

Many times, parents think they are not qualified to teach because they were not good at something in traditional school. Because of this, they think they need someone else to teach their children. But most of the time, it's simply a matter of learning alongside your child. I did not want to miss the opportunity to learn whatever my children were learning. Many times, I would get so excited to be learning whatever the children were learning that my husband said that he was sure our children would love to learn just from watching my excitement.

Funny NOW Story: I wasn't very creative, so I used a great unit study curriculum called KONOS, which gave me lists of ideas for activities to cover whatever topic we were studying at the time. One of the first unit studies we did was about light. In it was an experiment making rainbows on the wall by using a glass of water and a flashlight. (Keep in mind that I am color-blind, so I do not see color the way most people do.) Even though when I was in school I had memorized **ROYGBIV** - an acronym to remember the colors of the rainbow (red, orange, yellow, green, blue, indigo, and violet), I did not have a real understanding because I was never able to distinguish a rainbow's colors. Because of my inability to distinguish between colors, I waited until my husband was home to help with this experiment. Our oldest son is color-deficient too, but our oldest daughter can see color very well. I had two glasses of water and two flashlights. My husband was helping our son, and our daughter was helping me. The task was to create different rainbows on our white wall by shining a flashlight at an angle into the water. Then we were to list the colors in order on a piece of paper. No matter how many rainbows we created, the colors were always in the same order. For the first time in my life, I realized that God had created the rainbow so that the colors are always in the same order. I got so excited and realized my excitement had spread to my children as well. Infect your children with a love for learning as you learn alongside them.

Myth 10: *Parents cannot educate struggling or special education learners*

TRUTH: **Parents are capable of taking ownership of their struggling learner's education and are able to do so with great success.**

In the early days of homeschooling, parents of struggling learners were sometimes pressured to put their struggling students in traditional school. Now I often hear a parent say that a school recommended they homeschool so the student will get more one-on-one attention.

It has been my experience that no one will advocate and care for your child's education more than you. You may not know all the resources or answers, but you will strive to find the needed help. Many parents I talk to have given up their jobs to spend countless hours by their child's side to teach them life skills in an effort to help their child have as productive a life as that the child is able to obtain.

You may remember Dorothy saying, "There is no place like home." This is the truth. Parents regularly tell me that within a short time of bringing their child home, their behavior, concentration, happiness, and peace improved. Parents say, "I have a new child." In a home environment, education can be much more successful. Not one of us learns well in an environment of fear, anxiety, stress or anger.

My love for all my children, and especially a daughter with learning challenges, drove me to find whatever I could to help them succeed. I agree that it is great to have help, resources, therapies, and more, but parents know their children best, love them the best, and will advocate for them to get those services in a safe and nurturing way. Parents should oversee the education of their struggling learners.

Myth 11: *Parents should make educational decisions based on what the student wants.*

TRUTH: **Parents have the final say on educational decisions based on what the parent thinks is best for their child.**

I have lost count of the number of upset parents who have called me because their child wants to go back to public school. Many of the parents did not agree with the idea, but thought they had to give the child what they wanted anyway. One mom was literally yelling at me like I should be able to stop it.

I was asked one year what I would want to focus on and name my next workshop. I answered, *"Who is in Charge at YOUR House Anyway?"*

HELLO – If a child wanted to live on their own at age twelve, any parent in their right mind would set them straight pretty quick and tell them "NO!" We might discuss that they were not old enough, or that they don't have enough decision-making abilities yet to make that kind of life-changing decision for themselves. This world has tried to demote parents to the job of keeping their children happy and providing things their children want.

Children are to obey their parents so they will live long on the earth. Why do you think they will live long on the earth? Because parents are there to protect them, warn them when danger is around and train them in the truth.

Parents have been brainwashed into thinking that happy children will make happy adults. This is not true. Life is tough and they will not get everything their way in life. Most of the time what parents will end up with is a spoiled human being who thinks that it is everybody else's job to keep them happy. Maybe this is a contributing factor as to why society has an epidemic of self-centeredness these days. It's better to let children learn to accept "no" as an answer so they can learn these life lessons while they're under your roof and you can be there when they fall to encourage them to get up.

REMEMBER: Your job is not to make your children happy and to keep them liking you. It is to raise them to be adults. You are accountable before God to raise up your children in the way they should go to the best of your ability.

CHAPTER 2

Myths about Educating Children

Myth 12: *Teaching and Learning are the same.*

TRUTH: Going through the motions of some "teaching" method does not mean that students are learning. People learn more by using ALL of the senses they have.

This picture made me laugh; but, it has some sobering reality. What is the difference between teaching and learning? Sometimes there is a big gap between the two. We may be working hard through those workbooks and resources but that does not mean there is learning going on. Many moms I talk to clearly understand the difference between teaching and learning well because of the one-on-one method homeschooling provides. And sadly, other parents struggle to understand or have difficulty realizing the difference. They may know their child is miserable at school and never question the methods being used. Instead, they blame it on the child's lack of abilities or an unwillingness to learn.

Trust your heart! If your child is miserable and learning is challenging, consider if more time is needed to master concepts. Then, take the time necessary to change the resources and do whatever will work for your individual child. It does not matter how your child learns; so, do what is best for your child even if no one else is doing it that way.

One great way to bridge the gap between teaching and learning was by using a unit study approach. This is where you hook subjects together based on topics. After using this approach for years, I can develop a unit study out of just about any topic. Praise God, there were some great unit study writers that came before me who took their wonderful ideas and put them into a curriculum for me to follow. The unit study curriculum we used was called **KONOS** by Jessica Hulcy, which is still available today. I am sure by the time we went through all three volumes of **KONOS** we had covered every period of history, every area of science, many arts and music forms, theater, public speaking, physical activities (including Indian dances and horseback riding), Biblical history, and lots of literature using movies, audiobooks and library books. We also did a lot of field trips to tie the learning to real life jobs and occupations.

Funny NOW Story: One particular topic we studied in a unit study was on Indians. For Geography, we located on a map where major North American Indian tribes had lived. (The Internet now has interactive Indian Tribe Maps).

Map of Major
North American Indian Tribes

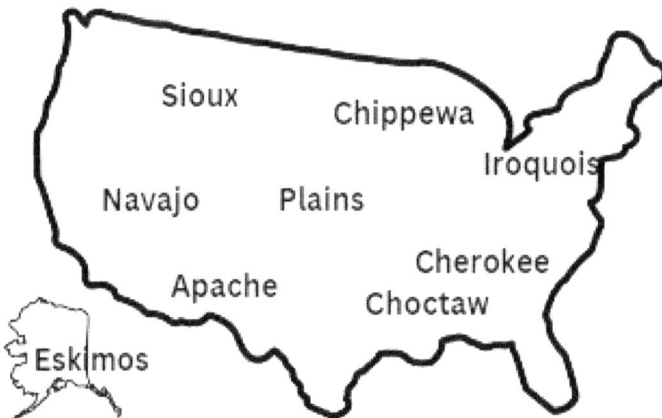

Our map had seven of the most well-known Indian tribes. We learned about one tribe at a time as we explored each of those areas of the country where the tribe lived.

- What were their houses built out of?
- What kind of animals lived there, especially ones they could use for food and clothes?
- How did they tan leather?
- What did they eat?
- How did they cook and preserve food?
- How did they make or dye their clothes?
- Did they weave blankets?
- How did they make geometric shapes through weaving?

We also learned about their music. For physical education, we went to an Indian pow wow and learned to do Indian dances. And of course, we read Indian stories and watched Indian movies along with writing and drawing about Indians. Each of my children designed their own homemade Indian outfit and headdress. With all those activities, we covered social studies, science, art/crafts, music, literature, and writing, along with other life skills.

The sad part was that before doing this unit study I thought every Indian lived in a teepee. I learned along with my children that the Indians were very smart, resourceful people who knew how to use everything around them. How their homes were built was dependent on what was available in their surroundings and whether they stayed in one place or if they needed to move around.

Unit study curriculum typically provides long lists of activities from which you can pick and choose what fits your time, budget, and energy. Many times, I would see an idea suggested. If I didn't have the resources needed for that idea, the idea would trigger another idea of something similar that was available that we could use instead.

Another reason I chose a unit study approach to learning is that I could do a unit study with one child, or several children, and I could adapt it to different learning styles. One child might be good at the analytical science part. Another child might be artistic and be able to draw maps or create costumes if they wanted to dress up. This allowed me the opportunity to discover talents and gifts unique to each of my children.

Funny NOW Story: When we were just getting started working with other families doing unit studies, I was doing a co-op in Pennsylvania where there was a boy who was somewhere between ten and twelve years old. He was the first child I had ever heard of diagnosed with ADHD. As we were getting together to plan what unit studies we would do for that school year, other parents kept mentioning that they didn't know how it was going to work out with this boy. (I think they were mostly concerned because he had not been able to thrive in a sit-down and be-quiet school situation.) However, I knew that the attention span of a child is about one minute for each year of their age. Much beyond that time and I would lose their attention. So, I planned co-op time to keep moving and not be like a classroom.

Understanding that most experiments are designed to figure out something, it is best to not tell the students what they are looking for or how to achieve the outcome. This develops problem solving skills. It's not about the product; it's about the process. The thing that amazed me was that this group of students might be working on a science experiment and this child with ADHD would be the one that would figure out how to make it work.

One experiment I specifically remember was about a unit study on architecture. Each student was given a half sheet of regular paper and challenged to build a bridge to go between two stacks of books. This bridge also had to be able to hold pennies. Most of the students looked at me like I had lost my mind. And to be honest, I would have had no idea about how this worked, but I had the answer in the **KONOS** book. Then I noticed this child with

ADHD begin to fold the paper like an accordion and place it on the books. We were all shocked when he was able to place several pennies on his bridge. We asked him how he figured this out and he said he just thought about bridges he had seen.

It showed me how we could use unit study learning to find the gifts and talents in students that may be hidden behind behavioral challenges or reading, writing, or math difficulties. I have learned that God has definitely given each child their own giftings. People don't have to be good at everything, they just need to excel at the special something that God put them on Earth to do. I love to go find and put that spotlight on their gift. We tend to put the spotlight on what a student is not good at doing. Instead, let's find out what they are good at doing.

Interacting with other families in co-ops using unit studies works really well. I enjoyed developing co-ops with families where we would get together once a week. All the work of planning and finding resources wasn't on one parent. We worked together and it was very economical. Doing unit studies in a co-op gave us the best of both worlds. We had some traditional education where we might do workbooks for math and language arts, and then we would do these unit studies where it was very hands-on and interactive. Our co-op days might have been described as organized chaos.

This is just one way to bridge the gap between teaching and learning. The important truth is to make sure whatever method of education you choose is bridging the gap between teaching and learning.

Myth 13: *Children learn best through reading, lectures, and tests because traditional schools do it best.*

TRUTH: Commonly found educational statistics show that using hands-on activities, audiovisual presentations, field trips, demonstrations, and having students verbally tell you what they know increases retention of information far beyond the reading, testing, and lecturing method of education.

Because of my background in cost accounting, I look at almost everything and ask, "Is it worth the time, money, and energy that will be spent? Is it producing the desired product or outcome?" So of course, I began to look at some statistics about education and what I found was very eye opening. Here is one of many research study pyramids that shows that reading and lecturing produces a very small amount of retention of information in the long term:

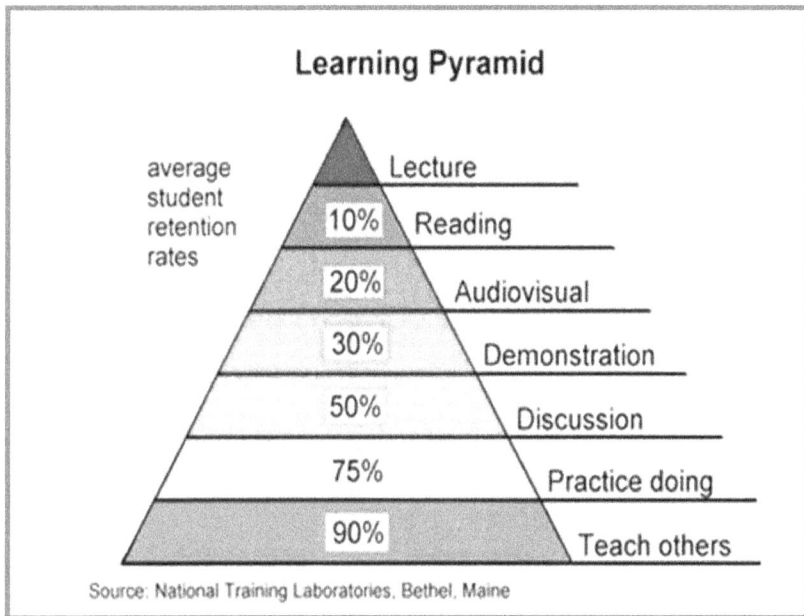

Learning Pyramid

average
student
retention
rates

10%	Lecture
	Reading
20%	Audiovisual
30%	Demonstration
50%	Discussion
75%	Practice doing
90%	Teach others

Source: National Training Laboratories, Bethel, Maine

I was shocked because I thought the "professionals" should know about these well-published statistics. Statistics show over and over that if students are just reading, taking tests and being lectured to, the long term retention of that information or learning will be 10% or less. What? How could this be? Almost all education is based on reading, testing, and lecturing.

These statistics explained a lot. Even though I was "successful" with traditional education by most standards, as I began learning with my children, I realized that I hadn't retained a lot of what I was taught. This realization was an eye-opening moment for me.

Funny NOW Story: When homeschooling CHILD 1 in first grade, we were reading a first grade American history textbook. As we read along, I didn't know many of the simple facts about American history. I looked at my husband who was in the room and asked him, "Did I even go to school? How did I miss this interesting information?" I realized that I must have been a great A maker when I was in school. I literally had to redeem my education as I homeschooled my children. I must admit the realization that I did not retain much from my traditional education really made me facepalm.

Myth 14: *Parents are raising children*

TRUTH: We are supposed to be raising Adults, NOT children.

We don't say that we are raising a corn plant or a blueberry bush. We say we are raising the product we want at the end of our efforts. We raise corn or we are raising blueberries. I did not want children in big bodies when I finished educating my children. I wanted ADULTS. It wasn't that I wanted them to act like adults as children but everything we do as parents should be part of watering, nourishing and preparing our children for adulthood. Just turning eighteen does not make someone an adult, but it can make for a very scary result when a person has rights to act and make decisions as an adult, but rather is still selfish and self-centered like a child. A capable person who still looks to others to provide for their needs and wants typically has no desire to learn, no work ethic, and no ability to problem solve. In my opinion, the idea that everybody deserves a trophy is a breeding ground for narcissism.

Funny NOW Story: I graduated from high school with a girl who had never turned on a washing machine. I assume somewhere along the way she learned to do laundry because she is now a mother and grandmother. I have

67

had college students visit my home that I have taught to do laundry, dishes, and other household chores and maintenance. These students told me that they were never allowed to do those things at home.

I was good at cleaning the house and laundry when I moved out on my own, but realized I hadn't learned to cook because my mom really didn't want us messing up her kitchen. All I knew about cooking was from observing my mom, but I didn't have much experience in the kitchen. I had to get help from my husband and friends to expand the menu options at my home. Today, my husband and children are still more creative cooks than I am. I did end up cooking three meals a day for twenty years, but I could have been better prepared.

When my two oldest children were still little, I had a neighbor with two sons that were finishing up college. One day when we were talking, she made a comment that stuck with me ever since. She said, "My sons have wonderful college degrees, but are not fit to be husbands. I did everything for them, and they even brought their laundry home from college. And now they really don't know how to live on their own. Their wives will have to do everything for them." I decided that day that was not going to be true of my children, especially my sons. I wanted my future daughter in-laws to rise and call me blessed for raising boys that would know how to do adult things.

It has been fun to watch my children teach their friends to cook, can fruits and vegetables, sew, mow grass, and the list goes on and on. Some of our children have actually come back and thanked us for letting them have the opportunity to learn how to do so many different things. At the time they may have thought it was "work," but now they realize we were preparing them to be adults.

REMEMBER: YOU ARE RAISING ADULTS, NOT CHILDREN

YOU WILL WANT ADULTS WHEN YOU ARE FINISHED.

Myth 15: *Parents need to make sure their children's lives are easy and better than their lives were.*

TRUTH: Like a weightlifter's spotter, parents are to allow adversity to strengthen their children while they are there to guide them.

Parents are supposed to train their children in the way they should go and that doesn't happen when life is easy. It is better to let your child learn hard lessons as they are growing up in the "greenhouse" of your home than to face the hard reality of life without any training. In this life we will have trouble. In real terms, life is a war, and we are soldiers. It would be awful to send people into battle with no training in how to fight. We must train our children academically, socially, emotionally, and most of all spiritually.

My children who went through the toughest things are my most understanding and caring adults. This does not mean that they are not tough and resilient. This does not mean they are a push over and won't stand for what is right. Quite the opposite is true. They will unselfishly stand up against adversity with a strength that amazes me, especially if they are protecting someone else. They have compassion and watch out for others' needs with hearts of love that they have felt from our heavenly Father when they went through tough things. God uses adversity in our children's lives to make them strong, like a butterfly that struggles to get out of the cocoon. If out of compassion someone helps a butterfly out of the cocoon to save it from the struggle, it will soon die because it is not strong enough to fly.

Remember: Don't be afraid of the tough things your children go through. Instead, look at it as God preparing them for something special.

Myth 16: *You have to push children to get them to achieve their maximum potential.*

TRUTH: Given the right environment for their learning style, children are natural sponges for information. Pushing and demanding because of high expectations can stunt a child's natural learning strength. Finding the learning style that fits your student is well worth it. More intensity doesn't mean a better education.

When homeschooling, you can keep it simple. Don't make it complicated. If you are stressed out and stressing out your children, they're not going to be learning to their full potential. None of us learn very well when we are under high stress and in tears.

People tell me, "My child cried through that reading lesson or math lesson." As a parent and teacher, I couldn't have my kids crying all day. If they weren't getting it, I just figured this wasn't the right way for that child to grasp what we were trying to accomplish, even if that method worked for an older child. Most children want to learn, but you may need to find a different plate on which to serve each child's unique education. Some children seem to learn fine off the traditional education plate.

I have also seen students pushed so rigorously because of what some people think is needed to go to college. The students become very stressed out, overachieving adults, or they just decide they are done and give up. More intensity does not mean a better education.

Myth 17: *ALL MY CHILDREN WILL LEARN THE SAME*
I should be able to use the same curriculum, method, and teaching style with all my children because I saved the curriculum from my other children.

TRUTH: All children are unique individuals, and their educational needs will be unique to them.

I love this picture of a house. There are so many

entry points. Over the years I began to see my children as being like houses. Let me explain: With Child 1, I could just walk near his front door, and he sucked information in. I thought this was going to be a breeze. I mean, he was learning stuff before I ever thought about teaching it to him. It was super easy. If he had been our only child, I would have thought that I was the greatest homeschool mom on the planet and everyone should just do it like me. However, God sent Child 2 to bless me with some humility.

Child 2 just did not want to learn anything that wasn't her idea. It was very hard to get her to open up her house. Until she wanted to open a door or window of her house, it was locked shut. She refused to learn her letters or numbers no matter how hard I tried. Then one day she decided she wanted to read with her brother. In one afternoon, she told me her entire alphabet and in a few short weeks she was reading with us. She wouldn't learn her numbers until she wanted to run the microwave like her brother. Again, before the day was out, she knew her numbers. I think she knew a lot of this all along, but it had to be in her timing and on her terms.

When she was in the second grade, she told me that she didn't think she needed a teacher but thought she could figure it out on her own. I suggested to her that she had never been in second grade before, but that I had, so I might be able to help her along the journey. And for a few more years she let me put things in her house without too much of a struggle.

Child 3's house was on wheels. He was always moving. When I could slow him down, he would very kindly let me put multiple things in his house. He learned best if more than one door was open at a time. He is a natural born multitasker who seemed to learn best if he was doing more than one thing at a time. For example, he would know every answer to a book I was reading as long as he could be playing with Legos at the same time.

Child 4 was calm after the whirlwind of Child 3. She pretty much opened all her windows and doors easily. She was reading by age four and again made me feel like I knew something about education. The challenge was that she struggled pronouncing polysyllabic words. We made no big deal out of it and just repeated words back correctly. Eventually she realized that if she set her mind to it, she could learn those words. When she was about fifteen years old, she came home from a homeschool class and said that she had problems saying big words. I reminded her that she was always able to conquer them, and she agreed. This daughter went on to learn big medical words in her nursing career.

Child 5 wanted you to put things in her house, but her doors were stuck. Most of the time, I would have to jump down the chimney or come up through the basement or somewhere else to get information into her house to find something that worked for her. Then she learned to help us find what worked to get her doors of learning open. Many resources I suggest today were found with her help. As an adult, this child has gone far beyond anything we could have imagined in those younger years.

Child 6's house seemed to have a timer system. At times his doors were open wide. He cooperated easily with learning and learning would come easy to him. Then there were times that every entrance to the house was locked shut and there wasn't anything penetrating that house whether he wanted it or not. This was very challenging until we realized that he thrived best with a lot of structure and routine.

Every child is different. Even when they come from the same parents, each child will need the parents to try different ways to access that individual child's learning house.

CHAPTER 3

Myths About Educational Environments and Settings

Myth 18: *You must have your student sitting at a desk doing seatwork at least 4 hours a day to count as school because kids are in school 7-8 hours a day being taught.*

TRUTH: Students don't have to be sitting at a desk at all to get a great education.

We have been led to believe our children will learn best if they sit still in desks, lined up in rows, while someone stands at the front of a class lecturing to them so they can pass tests based on what someone else thinks is important. But for years, statistics have shown that in the typical traditional school day of six periods, teachers have about 5-10 minutes per period to impart information to a classroom of students. This means that in a whole school day, students are only exposed to about 30-60 minutes of instruction. That means that in five days of science classes, the teacher would have about 25-50 minutes to attempt to educate. So don't be surprised when it takes much less time to accomplish far more education in the homeschool environment. Since our time with our children is not limited to a school schedule, we can consider the world to be our classroom. Most parents aren't going to miss an opportunity to make everything an educational experience. In addition, children are like sponges soaking up information. From the minute our children wake up until they go to sleep is education time; learning never stops. This revelation is why I didn't worry about days of attendance or how many hours I taught each day. I knew my worst day of homeschooling was better than the best day in a traditional school because education was continuous.

Myth 19: *We must have a classroom that looks like a public or traditional school.*

TRUTH: The world is the homeschool classroom.

With my traditional school mindset, I had a picture of what I thought our homeschool needed to look like. I thought it needed to be set up just like a regular classroom. There needed to be a teacher's desk in the front of the room from which to lecture, and my children needed to be sitting at school desks with books and workbooks. There should be posters on the wall with bulletin boards and a chalkboard too. I had even taken an educational class in college on how to create attractive bulletin boards. I thought all of that would make it a "real" school and that it was what I needed to do if I was going to homeschool my children. Believing this myth can become a really big hindrance because parents tend to think they can't homeschool without this set-up.

In reality, our "school room" was everywhere - from the dining room table to the picnic table - depending on what we were doing. If I was working with more than one child, we might read together on the couch or on the swing outside. We could go to the park or travel in a car and use a game to practice spelling words. Our school room ended up being a place to store books, supplies, games, and toys. Our one school desk was where a child had to do their schoolwork if they misbehaved. We worked school around our life instead of trying to work life around our school.

Funny NOW Story: One day my husband came in while I was reading to the children. I was sitting in a big recliner, nursing a baby and there was a child on each arm of the chair along with one on each side of my head on the back of the chair. My husband laughed and said, "You just need one on top of your head to complete the picture." Laughing is a big part of homeschooling.

Myth 20: *Students need books, workbooks, and tests to be a "real" school.*

TRUTH: Life experiences lead us to books and books lead us to life experiences. We ARE looking for real education.

At first, I did everything to set up my homeschool in a way that looked like a traditional school. I had my children up by 7:00 a.m., dressed and fed in time to start school by 8:00 a.m., when the workbooks came out and the schedule we adhered to began. Math at 8:00 a.m., English at 9:00 a.m., Science at 10:00 a.m., and Social Studies at 11:00 a.m. Lunch at noon. In the afternoon, we circled back to finish up anything that was not accomplished in the morning. We completed the assigned workbook pages and checked every box of work required for each day. HOWEVER, for all that work we did, I didn't see any light bulbs turning on for my children. They were just regurgitating information out of books and workbooks. Then I ran across a little book called the "Backyard Scientist" which gave ideas for science experiments that could be done by using things around the house.

At this time, we were living in married student housing at Bible college. It so happened that, about the time we were doing these science projects, the other kids were coming home from traditional school. So, they would stop by to play with my children. As we would do these hands-on science projects, I would see all the kids' eyes light up with wonder and excitement. They began to ask questions and figure out better ways to make the project work. I finally realized this was real education and that what was missing was a way to teach my children to think for themselves and become problem solvers.

REMEMBER: Real education teaches a child how to think, create, and learn.

Myth 21: *Kids need to have classes five days a week.*

TRUTH: Learning happens all the time, so classes can take place on the schedule that works for you.

Did you know that you don't have to do every subject every day? I think there are some big disadvantages to having classes spread over a five-day week. Let's think about what it would look like if a student went into a science class one morning a week for three hours instead of fifty-five minutes. Imagine if the teacher only had to take the role once in those three hours. She would have time to teach, incorporate experiments, hand-on projects, audiovisual aids, and sometimes maybe even have time to take the students on a field trip on that one day a week. This would be so much better than hopping from class period to class period for a five-to-ten-minute lesson. Even with this extended class period, teachers have no time for any kind of one-on-one remediation. It's just beyond their capability. There's just not time to do so in that system.

With the flexible schedule of home education, you can do one subject a day, take the time to make sure the child learns the relevant information, and plan field trips. In addition, with the wide variety of resource options available today, you have the opportunity to give your child a much better education in a home learning environment.

Did you know that you don't have to do every subject all school year long? You can do English and Social Studies in the Fall, Science and Health in the Spring, and math all year. You can plan your school year however it works for you and your family. We liked to plan school around our life, rather than our lives around school.

PLAN SCHOOL AROUND YOUR LIFE, NOT YOUR LIFE AROUND SCHOOL.

— MARGIE ABBITT

Funny NOW Story: I want to go back to Child 3, the multi-tasker - my Energizer Bunny boy. He is a real high energy person, as you might guess from his nickname. He would get up in the morning with more energy than most of us would have in a whole week. As he got older, I realized that it was probably not fair to ask anybody with that much energy to sit down at a table at 8:00 o'clock in the morning. As a matter of fact, he used to go out and chop firewood in the morning for fun. We lived in Ohio for sixteen years in a house that had a wood cookstove that heated our house, so we needed a lot of firewood. It was a blessing Child 3 loved to chop firewood.

One day, when he was about thirteen years old, he told me, "I need a job. You don't have enough wood for me to chop. I need something else I can do to stay busy."

Not long after that, we were attending a graduation party, and I was introduced to a family that was interested in homeschooling. I asked the father what he did for a living. He said that he ran a tree service. I asked how old someone needed to be to work for him. And he said, "Well, I don't really care how old they are. I care that they will work." When I told him that my son chops firewood for fun, he looked at my son and said, "You have a job. Show up on Monday."

Our son ended up working for this gentleman all the way through high school. Child 3 would go to work at about 7:30 in the morning and he'd come home around 2:30 or 3:00 in the afternoon. He did all his homework later in the day. Now, don't think he wasn't getting any "schooling" during that day, because he was.

About a year into this job, the owner asked Child 3 to go to an Arborology Convention. I thought that sounded like science. So, I started asking my son what he was learning. He knew the names of trees, diseases of trees, chemicals you use on trees, machinery for moving and planting trees, where to plant trees, where not to plant trees, and what not to put around the base of trees. Plus, he was going to these specialized conventions. I ended up giving him a science credit for high school in Arborology because he could tell us more about trees than anybody else I knew. This experience also ended up being a supplemental income for him in his adult life, even though that didn't become his career. He will never forget what he learned during that time.

Because of his multi-tasking abilities, he was able to handle a very full schedule, which included doing one subject each day of the week to get his academic work done while still having time to do martial arts in the evenings, Young Marines once a month, and Explorers with the fire department on Sunday afternoons. My Energizer Bunny boy could handle doing a lot of stuff.

Of course, not everyone is wired to handle a schedule like that. Some kids would not function well and need a slower pace of life. The point is that you can educate in the mornings, evenings, afternoons, or weekends - whatever works for your family's schedule.

Many families travel, play sports, own businesses, or may be professional singers or actors, and need this flexibility. Students may want to do schoolwork on the days while they're traveling. Then, when they get where they're going, be able to enjoy the fun. This also helps students learn to manage their time.

Remember: One of the beautiful things about home-schooling is your family's schedule does not have to look like anyone else's schedule.

Myth 22: *Children need to sit quietly and pay attention to the assigned task to learn.*

TRUTH: Children can be active doing other tasks and still be paying attention and learning as well.

When I think of traditional schools, I think of desks, tables, chairs, carpet squares, and learning centers. But, as we have discussed with home education, the options are anywhere: the kitchen table, the picnic table, couches, recliners, in the car, at the park, field trips, and even at grandma's house. Again, let's talk about CHILD 3. People would say to me, "I think he's ADHD." But I didn't think so. If I gave him a container filled with thousands of Legos, he would play for hours. His bedroom would be filled with the Lego creations he built.

When I would sit down to read a book with the children, I would have him sit next to me so I could keep an eye on him because he was always into something if he wasn't playing with Legos. As I would read, I would ask questions and CHILD 3 would not be able to answer even the simplest questions. I knew he was having trouble sitting still, but he was struggling to do so. Finally, probably out of desperation, I decided to just put the big container of Legos on the floor near me to keep him entertained since he wasn't getting anything out of the reading anyway. I figured that way, at least I would know where he was and what he was doing. I began to read and ask questions as he sat there building, and he began to answer every single question. I realized then that he is a multi-tasker and that when he sat next to me, all his energy and thoughts were going into sitting still and trying to stay out of trouble. He did much better if he was doing more than one thing at a time. I wonder now if he could have gotten this from me, because I'm a multitasker as well. I seem to think better, pay attention better, and I am more motivated if I am juggling more than one thing at a time.

This may be something you see in your own children that may make you frustrated. But realize that they may *need* to be doing more than one thing at a time. It is interesting that someone has come out with fidget toys and that many kids focus better if they are fidgeting with something while focused on their studies. All this reminded me of my genius older brother. When he was a young man, he bounced his leg a lot, which seemed annoying to others. But now I think it helped him focus better and use up excess energy.

Funny NOW Story: I remember one time when we were in a Sunday night church service and CHILD 1 had gotten tired and laid down on the pew. We thought he was asleep, until the pastor mentioned something and our son sat up and said, "Is that true?" I can't remember what the topic was, but I was astonished that he was listening even though he was not sitting up and facing forward.

Remember: Your children are paying attention a lot more than you think or realize. They are picking up and absorbing all the time, both the good and the bad.

Myth 23: *Every school day needs to look the same.*

TRUTH: Variety and the willingness to be flexible will lead to excited and engaged children; how boring life would be if every day was the same.

We learned to work school around our life instead of working our life around school. Life never looked the same from day to day, week to week, or year to year. Every day was a school day, but we didn't use books every day. Our children typically knew at the beginning of the week what was expected of them. They could choose to complete their work one subject a day, every subject every day, or finish all the work early in the week and have time for something special later in the week.

Many people have these wonderful little chore charts so that every day the children get stickers for doing their assigned chores. For many families this is very effective. However, this did not work for our family. The chores that were needed could change from day to day depending on what messes had occurred. Because each child had different abilities, I could not find a standardized way to get household responsibilities designated. Then, I came up with a simple list method. I would take a sheet of paper and write each child's name and my name. Under each person's name, I would list what they needed to do that day based on what needed to be done and according to their abilities. This way each one, like with the chart system, knew what was expected of them and they learned to manage their time in getting their responsibilities accomplished.

I considered that learning these life skills was just as important as reading, writing, and arithmetic. The one constant each day was that each person had their list of responsibilities to fulfill - before school, during school, and later in the day. When I realized every day would be different, and that was normal for my family, I was able to burn the super mom t-shirt, and my children learned work ethics in the process.

Schedules and routines can quickly become boring. In all my planning, I learned to create a rhythm in my home that worked best for my family, and that included flexibility and the freedom to focus on opportunities for fun and rest. It kept me and my family engaged and excited about learning. It also kept me from getting burnt out.

Remember: Routine has its purpose; however, all work and no play will drain the life out of learning.

Myth 24: *A student needs four or more hours of what looks like traditional school when learning at home.*

TRUTH: Learning at home can be done in a fraction of the time it takes to learn in a traditional school.

This myth starts with the idea that students are learning the entire time they are at school. The truth was revealed to me when I was faced with the challenge of developing a transcript for my first high school student, who was ahead of the game and doing high school courses at 13 years old. (**Note:** Not all of my children were ready for high school this early.) At this time the only homeschool parents I had met with high schoolers were writing the courses and grades on a piece of notebook paper. Being an accountant, I knew how to run a spreadsheet, I could figure GPA, and I had a printer in my home office. With these tools in my belt, I knew I could develop official looking transcripts. However, I needed to start researching what makes up a high school course and what counts as a credit. I knew I had gotten a transcript with credits for high school and college, but I wasn't quite sure what determined a credit, and I wasn't quite sure what that looked like for a homeschooler.

During my search, I ran across a book where a study had been done on what goes on in a high school course, including laying out transcripts. It had lots of information, but the statistic that stood out to me the most was a study of what goes on in high school classrooms. The study said that the average class period at that time was 55 minutes and that teachers only had about 5-10 minutes to teach in each of those class periods. Now, at first when I would say that at conferences, I figured somebody was going to buck that statistic. However, experienced teachers confirmed this, and many said they probably didn't even get that much time to teach their subject.

Let's do the math. This means that in a typical 5-day week of traditional science classes at 5-10 minutes per class period, a student might get 25-50 minutes a week to be taught on a given subject. That meant in the school day maybe 30 minutes to an hour may actually be used to contribute to sharing information to a classroom of students.

I wondered how students were able to succeed in that kind of environment. And then I realized that they are being home educated in the evenings. I remember a mom sharing that she spent hours in the evening doing homework with her daughter and even hired tutors to help her. I realized that I was homeschooling in the morning, and she was homeschooling at night. When I went to school, even though I was a highly motivated learner, I still had homework to do. I had to study and teach myself the information at night. It seems to me that it is just easier to home educate my children on our schedule.

With the right curriculum for the child, it would take a fraction of that 7-8 hours to accomplish much more than is accomplished in a traditional school schedule.

Myth 25: *Time is used efficiently to educate during the traditional school day. Educating at home will not be efficient.*

TRUTH: Time can be used more efficiently in the homeschool setting.

Let's stop and think about this one. Teachers are responsible for doing several logistical tasks, and many have to be done during each class period, like taking the role, handing out papers, taking in papers, and letting students go to the bathroom. This does not even cover how much time is lost when students are between classes.

Then there is the biggest problem to deal with: discipline. Just trying to keep the class under control and safe is becoming a bigger issue every day. Teachers have been stripped of the authority to give consequences for bad behavior, and in many cases have to be concerned for their own lives. I have utmost respect for teachers who assume these roles and truly want to make a positive difference in students' lives.

Teachers, also, have their hands full doing all the required paperwork and being forced to teach to tests. Many teachers are leaving the profession because this is not what drew them into teaching. They wanted to teach children, not teach to tests. More and more opportunities for educating in the homeschool world are emerging as long as these teachers can leave their doubly trained public school mindset behind them and embrace how children really learn.

When talking with families, the consensus is that a lot of time is wasted during a school day. Some parents will call and ask if they are doing something wrong because their child got done with their assignments so quickly. Homeschooling is just a more efficient way to educate children.

CHAPTER 4

Myths About Results and Expectations of Education

Myth 26: *If I replicate public school, I will get better results at home than at school.*

TRUTH: Replicating traditional school at home leads to the same frustrations that were encountered in the traditional school setting.

The indoctrination of this myth is very strong, but I think Albert Einstein's definition of insanity explains it well. "Insanity: doing the same thing over and over and expecting different results." Helping parents realize that doing traditional school at home will not create a different outcome from traditional school is often like trying to cut chains off a prisoner. It can be difficult to cut through all the links that are formed through our educational experiences.

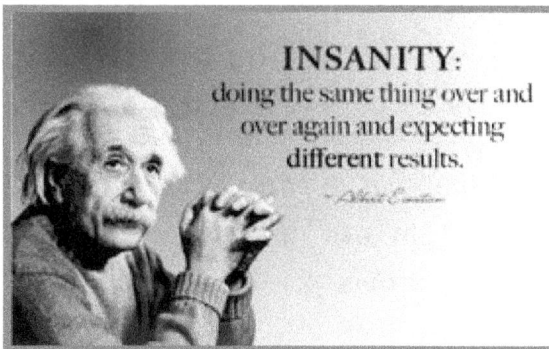

INSANITY: doing the same thing over and over again and expecting different results.
~ Albert Einstein

Homeschooling parents who were trained as traditional school teachers in college often struggle more to break free of traditional school mindsets. It has been my experience that accepting the freedom that is available to home-educators to educate in the way they think is best is the hardest for those with the highest degrees in education. So, if that is you, you may need to read this book a couple of times and watch my webinars. Most teachers, I would guess, went into teaching to teach children and got indoctrinated into teaching to tests, then lost that vision when it was more about teaching children to get ready for tests. Now, many teachers tell me that their jobs are more about keeping the children safe.

I would like to add that many parents see significant improvement in their student's attitude, behavior, and learning just by getting them out of the traditional school environment. Even if they take a traditional approach at home, the stress and pressure is decreased. It is okay if the change in educating your child is a step-by-step process. I have worked with some moms for two or three years, and they will say, "I finally get it. Not doing education like traditional school really works."

Myth 27: *If a student can read and take tests well, they are smart; if they can't read or take tests well, they aren't.*

TRUTH: "Smart" is different for different people. Each of us is smart in our areas of gifting and expertise. Homeschooling allows you to focus on what each student is smart at doing.

Every day, I hear parents refer to one of their children as smart and another as not being smart based on how they do at reading, doing math, and taking tests. I know they mean well, but I know these words come from the influence of a traditional education system.

Funny NOW Story: When I was young, my dad would tell me that when he was in the 11th grade, his school added the 12th grade. He would remind me that there weren't always 12 grades in school. His school thought that he should stay the extra year because he hadn't done so well the previous years. He would laugh and tell me, "I didn't learn any more that 12th year than I had in the 11 years before." I never saw my dad read much more than a newspaper and his Bible. However, my father was one of the smartest men I have ever known. He was a walking encyclopedia about machinery, appliances, water conditioners, and more. He could fix almost anything brought to him. When he was 68, my dad was more than ready to retire. The company he worked for did not want to see him go because he could design and build machines for their textile mills that their college-trained engineers had no idea how to do.

Even though my dad struggled in school, he still had the major qualities that are necessary for a successful life:

(1) He loved to learn. He was never afraid to try to learn anything he needed to know. When we would go to museums with old machinery or an aeronautical museum, I would see him taking a machine apart in his mind to figure out how it worked.

(2) He knew how he learned best. He was a visual and kinesthetic learner. He worked best when he was using his hands. And he understood schematics (diagrams) of machinery as well as any highly trained engineer.

(3) He had a great work ethic. He worked at least 2 jobs his whole life and always provided well for our family.

(4) He had a great attitude. He never gave up, even when his hand was crushed in an accident due to faulty machinery, and he subsequently lost his job. He proceeded to start his own appliance repair business, and then went to work for a textile company until he retired.

(5) He had problem-solving abilities. Having grown up during the depression, he knew how to take what others discarded and either fix it or turn it into something useful.

(6) He was very kind. He loved my mom and our family, and he provided well for us. He would find a way to help those who couldn't afford to pay what they owed him.

There are many other stories of his kindness. Above it all, he was a man of God who knew how to...

(7) Listen to and be led by God.
All these things contributed to his incredible "smartness."

REMEMBER: "SMART" should not be defined by a person's ability to read or to take tests well. Being smart goes much deeper than that. "SMART" could be defined as "excelling at one's abilities".

Myth 28: *We must have tests and grading scales in order to determine grades.*

TRUTH: Homeschoolers SHOULD get A's, and it is okay.

In my early years of homeschooling, people would ask me what "grading scale" I used to assign grades to my children. I was well trained in the public-school way of giving grades. It included giving tests and averaging test scores to give the infamous grade. However, some schools give an A if the average was 91 -100. In other schools, 93-100 might be an A, or 90-100, and so on.

None of this made sense to me, especially for a homeschooler. In the early grades, but even into high school, I began to realize that looking at tests for grades was all wrong as homeschoolers. Because most of us have experience with traditional school, we teach like homeschoolers and grade like a traditional school.

Let's first talk about K through 8th grades when a parents' main job is to teach their child to love to learn. Children learn best through experiential learning, field trips, games, etc., while having a lot of fun. It may seem hard to grade fun. So instead of letter grades, the grading should be something like Pass, Satisfactory, or Excellent. You don't need test scores because you are with your student. You know what your child knows and doesn't know. Most homeschool parents will go back over a topic if they realize their child hasn't learned something they may need to know. I call this "Remediate to Mastery". So, if your student masters the information, what grade do they deserve? They would receive an Excellent for their grade.

A web search on the statistics about Information Retention helped me understand how grading is different with home education versus traditional school.

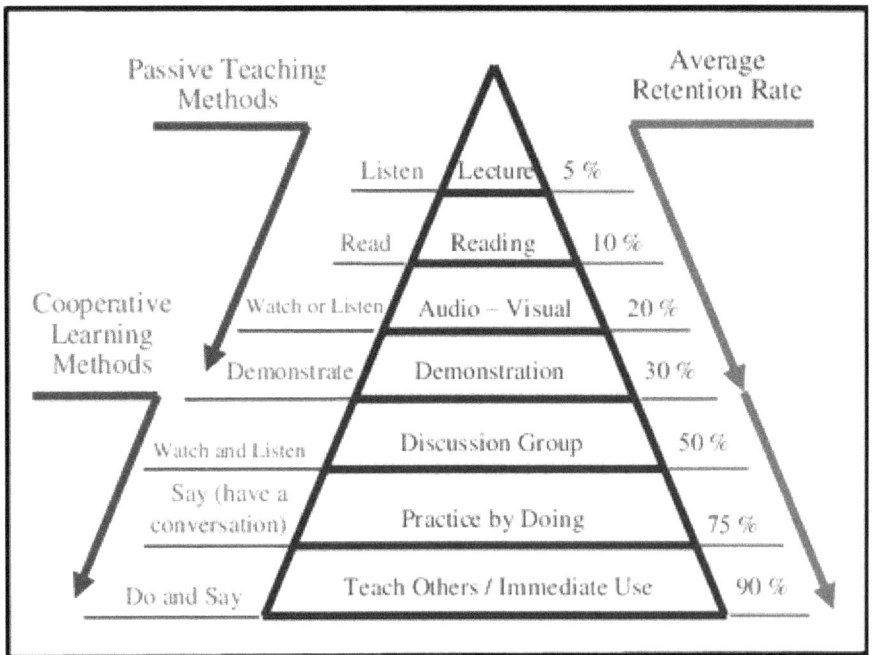

The learning pyramid diagram. On the left, Passive Teaching Methods transitioning to Cooperative Learning Methods; on the right, Average Retention Rate.

Passive Teaching Methods	Pyramid level	Average Retention Rate
Listen	Lecture	5 %
Read	Reading	10 %
Watch or Listen	Audio – Visual	20 %
Demonstrate	Demonstration	30 %
Watch and Listen	Discussion Group	50 %
Say (have a conversation)	Practice by Doing	75 %
Do and Say	Teach Others / Immediate Use	90 %

My synopsis was that, typically, if any student uses the education methods limited to reading, testing, and lecturing, those students retain about 5 to 10% of that information long term. It isn't much, but that is the way most education is presented, and then the students take a test on that material to get their grade. After giving several tests, teachers average the scores together and a final grade is given.

Homeschool offers an alternate way to look at grading because our assessment methods can be very different. For instance, I ask many parents what they do when their student gets something wrong on a test or when they know that their student doesn't understand something. The basic answer is always the same: "We go back over it until they get it." This is what makes the difference. You're doing mastery teaching or "remediating to mastery". This remediation is also called a one-on-one tutorial education, which can be provided with home education.

Funny NOW Story: Oftentimes in my homeschool journey, God put me in different places so that I would pick up information to help with my understanding of education. One of those times was in 1992, when I got the opportunity to go back to college and I took an Educational Psychology course that covered different ways to design classroom settings to increase learning. The last chapter in the textbook discussed how one-on-one tutorial education had proven to be the number one best way to educate any child. Using the textbook as my main point of reference, I decided to title my final paper for that class, "Homeschooling: The Number One Best Way to Educate any Child".

With a one-on-one tutorial education system, students can master information by going as fast or as slow as they need. If a curriculum is not working, we have the freedom to adjust or even discard it for better options. I also pointed out that students are allowed time to master any information that is relevant. Not all information in every book is relevant. I knew writing about this might be kind of risky in 1992, but I got an A on that paper. Amazingly, the professor agreed with me.

Consider a classroom of 15, 20, 30, or more students. There is little to no way the teacher will have time to give any student one-on-one attention. The way most traditional students succeed is if they are getting that one-on-one time when they get home from school, engaging in that thing called "homework." Parents of traditional school students need to go back over things at night when their child is tired after a long day of school. In home education, however, we give that one-on-one time whenever best fits the student's learning style. My heart goes out to the traditional schoolteacher who at best has gone over the topic, administered a test, and students get the grade they get. There's no time for mastery learning to be accomplished despite all the teacher's best efforts.

Final grades should be based on mastered concepts, not test scores. Parents who homeschool know what concepts their children have mastered and which ones are still developing because they can see the progress their children are making. When you let go of testing as the measure of learning, you can see that learning is happening and can take the time to assess their progress accordingly. Many times, home educators think that the grade received on a test, from a computer program, or from a co-op or class teacher is the final grade that must go into the child's records. But I believe the parent has the final say on the grade depending on whether remediation to mastery has occurred during the learning process.

I realized that homeschooling provided a totally different way to educate with one-on-one tutorial education, which allowed remediation to mastery. So why would we grade based on tests? Instead, we should use the tests only as needed to show us what might need to be remediated to mastery. When mastery is accomplished, of course, your student should receive an A for that accomplishment.

The exception is still not based on a test, but on the student's work ethic and attitude. If a student is rebellious and refuses to complete assignments, even when adjustments and accommodations are made for learning style, then a lower grade should be assigned.

Myth 29: *All information in the curriculum should be mastered.*

TRUTH: WATCH OUT! Curriculum contains a lot of interesting information, but only a small amount of the material, even though memorized for a test, will remain in long term memory and so it will not be mastered.

Your curriculum is a resource to give you ideas for what you might want to share with your children. Most curriculum comes with some kind of test, but not everything that is on a test is really worth mastering. Over those 30+ years of watching curriculum, I saw curriculum change.

I won't forget the day when I realized that CHILD 5's

new biology curriculum was requiring her to memorize the scientific names of algae. I knew there was nothing like that in our older children's biology books, and I also knew that even if we spent a week or two memorizing the scientific names of algae, no one would retain that information long term unless it was used on a regular basis. I was really questioning why this would be added to the curriculum and decided I was going to own this curriculum instead of it owning me. I told my daughter she was not going to memorize the scientific names of anything in high school and if she needed to learn them, she could learn them in college.

A science resource I found that kept information simple was *The 101 Series* produced by Westfield Studios, which has DVD courses in General Science, Biology, Chemistry, and Physics. The beauty of this series is that it just teaches what students need to know about the subject without the fluff. The lessons took about an hour a week, which left time for hands-on activities like experiments and field trips.

The rest of the story is that CHILD 5 enrolled in a biology-related major in college. She called home during her honors biology course to let me know that she was not even required to memorize scientific names of algae in college. We laughed as she seemed quite amazed that I had known not to make her do that in high school.

As I mentioned earlier, there seemed to be a lot of extra material my younger children needed to know that my older children hadn't needed to learn. I wanted to know why. God, in his faithfulness, sent me someone to answer my question about the extra information being added to textbooks.

I met a gentleman one day and asked him what he did for a living. He said he was a curriculum producer. I have never met someone before or since that told me that was their occupation. So, I figured this was a God thing and I would ask him my question. I explained how I had been seeing new things added to curriculum. He immediately said, "Oh, we have to do that in order to produce new versions of the book. You know, we have to add so much additional information in order to sell new editions."

"So, it's not because the students need to learn it, " I asked him, "but it's so you can make money?" I have to say that the man turned a little pale as he began to realize what was going on. I explained to him how confusing this is to students and parents who don't know what is relevant to learn and what is not.

After this encounter, I put 2 and 2 together and realized colleges have been doing this for a while. When I went to college, I normally only had to buy one book for a class. I could buy a used book and sell it back at the end of the semester. However, by the time my children got to college, professors were requiring the newest editions, and usually more than one book.

CHILD 4 began to comment that the professors were only covering certain parts of those expensive textbooks and much of the book went unused. CHILD 4 got smart. She would ask the professor which books on the booklist the class would really require and she would rent those textbooks for a fraction of the cost. Then she would return them at the end of the semester, and she didn't get stuck with a book containing a lot of useless information. Often the professor would tell her that the 1st edition of the book would include the information being covered in the class. I realized that the professors might be required to list the new books for their classes, but they probably knew what was important to teach the students; so, they just covered those parts of the newer editions.

Even if you must use a newer edition for a co-op or tutorial, you can use common sense to determine what your student really needs to learn for that subject. A good guideline to determine what to cover is whether you have ever needed to know that information in your adult life. You might want to let the teacher know that a newer edition probably is not a better edition.

I am sure there are exceptions to every myth I talk about. One exception I know for publishers to create a new edition is when the United States has had a few more presidents. Then a publisher will print a new edition to include them.

Try to get 1st editions of the curriculum, especially for core subjects like math, English, science, and social studies. Steer clear of 2nd, 3rd, and 4th editions listed as a resource. I even saw a 6th edition book listed once. I can only imagine how much would have had to be added or changed to get to a 6th edition. The newest edition is not necessarily better in the curriculum world. Own Your Curriculum! Don't Let Your Curriculum Own You.

REMEMBER: Over time, a lot of options have become available. We have to be careful because homeschoolers have become a marketplace. People like to sell to homeschoolers. Businesses know that we're out here. When I travel to homeschool events, I like to ask vendors, "How many children are you homeschooling?" Many times they will admit they don't homeschool and know little about homeschooling.

Myth 30: *Playing is NOT learning. Learning doesn't need to be fun. They are just playing, NOT learning.*

TRUTH: Play gives children the chance to practice what they are learning and opens doors to curiosity.

I have come to understand that we learn more and

retain more information when we're having fun. Imagine you are in a boring meeting and you find yourself thinking, "Oh please, I'm not even hearing what you're saying. I am so bored. Please don't let me fall asleep. When is this going to be over?" How much of the information are you really learning, or are you just enduring it?

"PLAY GIVES CHILDERN THE CHANCE TO PRACTICE WHAT THEY'RE LEARNING"

— MR. ROGERS

Funny NOW Story: When our grandson, who was under two years old at the time, was visiting, he picked up his plastic bowl off the table. He put it up next to his cheek and started saying, "Blah, blah, blah, blah." My first instinct was to tell him to put his bowl down. But then, all of a sudden, he picked up another bowl and put it up to the other side of his face. He started, "Blah, blah, blah" into both of them; first one and then the other. I realized he was listening to the sounds. Because the bowls were not the same size, they were giving him different sounds. He was just naturally learning about sound. This grandson

109

has loved music from a very young age, and I couldn't help but wonder what skills he was developing with what seemed to be just messing around with bowls. We want to watch for these learning opportunities rather than seeing them as something bad or making a mess.

Many times we do not see play as learning. But a huge part in enhancing learning is enjoying, laughing, and doing fun things in play.

Myth 31: *Learning Must be Serious.*

TRUTH: Play is a great way to Learn.

I personally don't think much of anything positive can be learned when we are bored, frustrated, sad, or angry. I believe these emotions put the brain into survival mode, so it is good if we can avoid them when trying to learn.

Funny NOW and then Story: For one year of physical science, I used a standard basic science book. But, instead of just reading it and taking the tests, I looked at the chapter titles and bold-faced words for topics to do experiments and take field trips. Some of the most hilarious things can leave the most lasting retention of information.

One of the experiments that we will never forget

was on air pressure. I searched the web for an experiment that went along with air pressure and found one that had us laughing until our sides hurt, but it got the point across. The experiment was that each student took turns standing in a big plastic lawn/leaf garbage bag and the student held the top of the bag snugly around their neck. Next step, the helper stuck a vacuum cleaner hose into the bag and turned the vacuum on. Immediately the air inside the bag was pulled out and the bag was snugly fitting around the person with a lot of pressure. Then, in between all the laughter, we would talk about what was going on. Where was the pressure coming from-inside or outside the bag? How did this compare to air pressure in an airplane? Information was retained more easily because it was fun.

REMEMBER: "Play is the highest form of research" by Albert Einstein.

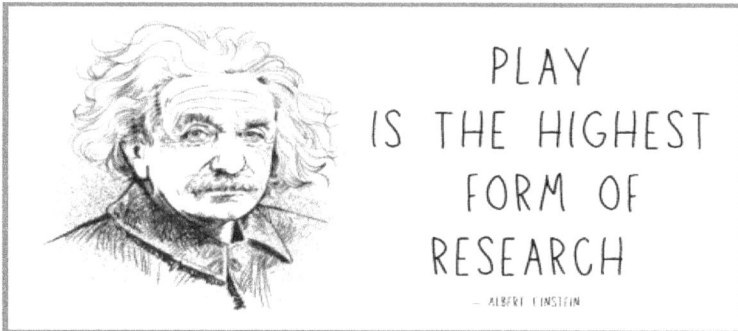

PLAY
IS THE HIGHEST
FORM OF
RESEARCH
— ALBERT EINSTEIN

CHAPTER 5

Myths About Curriculum

Myth 32: *All curriculum is created equal. Also, Christian private school curriculum is better because it has God in it.*

TRUTH: Curriculum is NOT created equal. Good Christian content does not mean the curriculum content will work well for your child.

When parents answered the call of God to start homeschooling in the 1970s and 1980s, there was NO curriculum written for homeschool or written by homeschoolers. Many homeschooling families turned to private Christian schools for curriculum options. Much of that curriculum still used the same read, test, and lecture system that the public schools used. Unfortunately, many homeschoolers were sucked into the idea of mirroring school at home rather than embracing the freedom to educate their children at home in the way that was best for them and their children. Some of us only stayed stuck a short time, but many homeschoolers are still stuck there today.

Of particular note, in the beginning, private schools did not want to sell us their books. I called to place an order from one of the big-name private school curriculum producers and had a representative say to me "You should realize schooling your own children is just a fad, and go ahead and put your kids in school."

Homeschooling has definitely proven not to be a fad. Those same private school curriculum producers caught on very quickly that they could make a lot of money by setting up the biggest booths at homeschool events. They promote themselves as an all-in-one package deal for curriculum with all their books, workbooks, and tests, which now have multiple editions. They may even offer "accredited" online programs. Sadly, I talk with parents every week that have been drawn into buying these expensive options and are miserable. Many times, they think they are failing at homeschooling and are ready to quit.

The problem is curriculum is formatted to fill up 180 days of school, with extra lessons and work just in case you get through it in under 180 days. Our goal should not be to fill up 180 days or to cross every "t" and dot every "i" in a workbook, but rather to give our children a great education to prepare them to do what God made them to do.

Fortunately, home educators started to design their own curriculum. Today there are a lot of options for curriculum designed for or by homeschoolers with freedom and flexibility in mind and with the purpose of covering a subject, not filling up 180 days. Keep in mind that "HOMESCHOOL" is now a marketplace and not everyone at a homeschool convention is there to promote homeschool, but just to sell a product. If you go to a homeschool convention, you might have some fun asking vendors if they homeschool their children.

REMEMBER: TWO MAJOR THINGS to keep your Freedom in Homeschooling:

1. Own your curriculum; don't let it own you.
2. Curriculum, resources, co-ops, tutorials, and computer programs are your tools, and you are in charge of how they are used and the grade that is given.

Myth 33: *Students must have textbooks, workbooks, computers, and access to the Internet to count as school.*

TRUTH: Learning comes from much more than textbooks, workbooks, computers, or the Internet. Learning comes from the REAL world.

Funny NEVER Story: At one time, I worked as a bookkeeper for a large corn farm in the Midwest. This is where I learned the term, "roguing corn." The goal for a

GMO crop is for all the corn to be the same height and produce the same number of ears of corn. Any corn stalk that grew too tall was "rogued" or pulled out of the field so it could not pollinate or affect the other plants. To me this was a picture of what the government schools want from our children and us – conformity or we might get "rogued."

Let's review the statistics I shared before. In the same research that showed us if you read and lecture for learning, it produces a 5-10% retention rate of information. It also shows that if a person hears it, sees it, does it, and talks about the material, retention of the information increases up to 90%. In other words, if children have hands-on projects, audiovisual learning, field trips and demonstrations, and can tell you verbally what they know, there is a 90% chance they will remember it long term.

I had to ask my very analytical, in-the-box self, "Do I want 10%, or do I want to change and aim for the 90%?" I determined that my children were worth getting out of the "GMO" box of traditional education, so I did education differently. **I was willing to buck the system and shoot for the 90%.**

Changing my method of homeschool education meant not educating like many other homeschoolers I knew at the time. However, I knew in my heart that I had to change how I was going to look at education in order to give my children a chance at the 90%. When we started home education, there was not a computer in every home and the Internet was unheard of. I was already homeschooling when educational VHS tapes became available at the library. We used real life. The science projects on the kitchen table were from real things around our home. We went on field trips to real places with real people to learn how they did real jobs. **The real world should be your first choice for education.**

After we read books, we found ways to experience what we had read about. When we were having real life experiences and wanted to learn more, we would go find books to learn more about what we had experienced. God gave us five senses (seeing, hearing, touching, tasting, and smelling). Learning is increased when we incorporate as many of these senses as possible. ALL OF THIS COUNTS FOR SCHOOL.

Myth 34: *All children need to read, write and do arithmetic well and early.*

TRUTH: Children will learn reading, writing and arithmetic at different ages and in different ways, and it doesn't always happen early.

When we were starting to walk away from traditional school ideas, we had a kindergartener and a 2nd grader and we were literally most concerned about what the basics of reading, writing and arithmetic were going to look like for our children. My grandmother used to say, "the important part of education you have to get is reading, writing and arithmetic." We had to go back to the basics and figure out what education was going to look like for each child. It became apparent, even with just two children, that not all children learn things at the same age. CHILD 1 was identifying letters at 2 and reading well at 4. CHILD 2 had no interest in learning anything that was not her idea to learn until she was ready to learn it. But as adults, no one really cares at what age they learned to read or how quickly they learned math facts. The brain develops differently for each child. CHILD 1 was very analytical (left brained) from a young age, but our second was very creative (right brained) from the start. Each one was very smart in their own way, but very different in their interests, abilities, and gifts.

Funny NOW Story: One day I was on the phone helping a very creative, right brained homeschool mom who told me that she loved to write. However, from her description I could tell she had a very left brained son who loved math and science. Mom wanted to stop the math and science in order to force this 11-year-old boy to learn to write creatively and wondered why it was affecting their relationship. She was set free when I pointed out to her that her son could have different strengths and to focus more on those. Typically, the other side of the brain will level out as the brain matures.

I didn't like to write in school. I could not understand why anyone needed 3 pages on a topic when I could tell you all I thought you needed to know in a paragraph. Now I am writing this book. Miracles can happen.

A child that loves math may struggle with reading, and a child that struggles with math may do much better at reading and writing. A child that likes art and music may need their education delivered in a way that involves musical and artistic activities. It is important to accept that students will learn different things at different times and in different ways. Reading is not the only way to learn, and learning to read doesn't always happen early.

Myth 35: *We have to have a curriculum in order to "count" as school.*

TRUTH: A lot of learning happens without curriculum. The best learning is messy, but it definitely counts as education.

119

I find humor in parents wanting to have a curriculum for their kindergartner so everything they do "counts" for school. You can let your children learn by doing, especially in the younger ages.

Let's talk about how learning comes naturally. Children are naturally curious learners, explorers, and adventurers. As parents, we may typically just consider them "mess makers". I have had times in my house that it looked like some of these pictures:

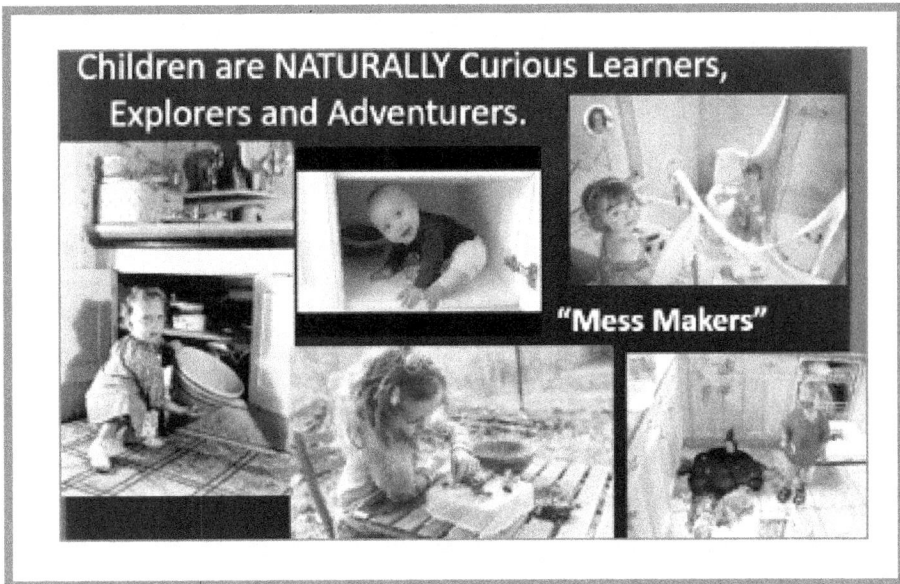

I have learned over the years to look at this differently. As frustrating as it can be that they have made a mess or they're not doing something the way you wanted, a lot of times it's out of their natural curiosity to learn that they are making messes. Our first reaction usually is to get upset because of the mess. Instead, we can choose to appreciate their curiosity and creativity and try to limit the mess as much as possible. To be forthright, this is where I taught them to ASK: "If you would like to play with that, please ask."

Funny NOW Story: Once I had a very upset neighbor lady who told me that her 11-year-old son was taking apart her small appliances, clocks, etc. I thought, "I do not want that to happen in my house" as I could imagine my kids taking things apart. I decided to get ahead of that game and give them things to take apart. Anytime something would break, I would save it. Then on days when we had extra time, I would put my broken treasures on the dining room table, give them screwdrivers, hammers, and different tools, like an ohm meter to test circuits. The kids, especially the boys, loved to get in there and take things apart. The interesting thing was that I could not teach them how to fix any of it, but they began to figure out not only how these things worked, but what was wrong. Sometimes they even completely repaired them. Their minds began to naturally learn how things fit together.

Some years later, we were at the Center of Science Industry (COSI) in Columbus, OH. They had just opened a new section where kids could take things apart like computers, appliances, old telephones, and lamps. My children looked at me and said, "We've been doing that on the dining room table for a long time."

This is a really good way to learn. It doesn't cost a lot of money to just have them take real things apart. When other people found out we did this, they would give us their broken stuff. It would even be worth it to spend a few dollars at the thrift store to get items to take apart. Some thrift stores may be willing to save you the things that have been donated that don't work. Our job as homeschool educators is to encourage their curiosity and to steer them toward purposeful learning opportunities. You can guide them while allowing them to explore. In this way, a love for learning is developed.

REMEMBER: All life experiences, whether hands-on or in a book, "count" for education when you homeschool.

Myth 36: *Games don't count as education.*

TRUTH: Board games, card games, computer games, outside games - games of many kinds - are all a means of education. Education is more fun when you don't know you are learning.

So many times, we think subjects have to be taught a certain way. We've got to have a particular workbook, or we've got to have a specific book. But it really doesn't matter. If it's a game that teaches them the desired material, then that is the resource for that subject.

I would watch to see if learning was taking place. One of the ways I knew learning was happening was when my children got excited and talked with me about what they learned. Games brought out a lot of excitement when they beat the levels. Many times, being successful in a game indicated their learning progress.

Funny NOW Story: One time, we were doing a world geography curriculum with my older high school children. Throughout the textbook they covered all the regions and continents in the same factual and methodical way, chapter after chapter after chapter. It went through each country on each continent and included information about the crops, population, flags, major cities, etc. The repetition was so boring that when I was trying to go through it with the kids, I kept falling asleep. If this was boring for me as an adult with a longer attention span, then what in the world must it have been like for my children?

I believe God saw my frustration and provided a solution. I found a free website that taught world geography by using beat-the-level games. In a very short period of time my older children could take a continent, name the countries, move every country onto it by shape, and put the topography on the maps. They learned more about world geography playing these games than I had ever learned in school. And they had more fun in the process.

Using games may also come in handy when you have children that struggle and need audiovisual and hands-on learning.   I encourage you to shift your traditional school mindset and be willing to do things that are out-of-the box so that your children can actually learn.

Remember: It doesn't matter **how** your student learns. It matters that your child actually learns.

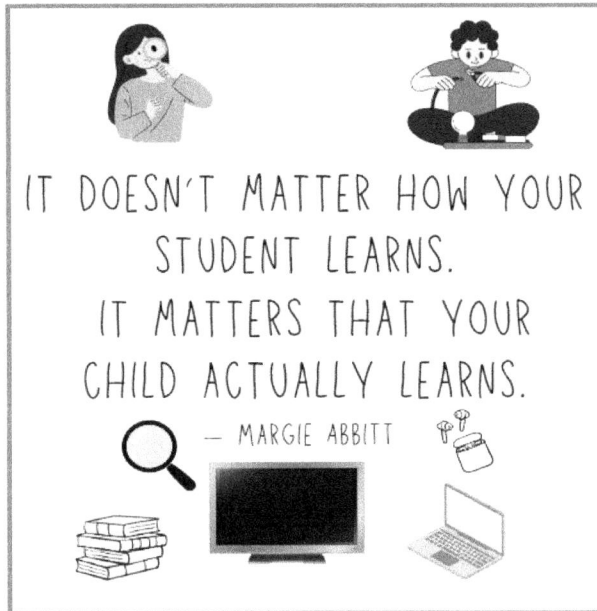

IT DOESN'T MATTER HOW YOUR STUDENT LEARNS.
IT MATTERS THAT YOUR CHILD ACTUALLY LEARNS.
— MARGIE ABBITT

Myth 37: *I must follow a Scope & Sequence like the traditional school to make sure I don't miss anything.*

TRUTH: A Scope & Sequence limits the flexibility of each child's learning styles, interests, or abilities. Education should be based, not on grade level, but on a readiness to learn.

First, let me explain Scope & Sequence. It is a term used to describe a tool educators use that lays out what ideas and concepts will be taught and when.

The Scope & Sequence method is used to help traditional education systems keep up with what they need to teach and still have to cover. My traditional education mindset assumed that students couldn't learn states and capitals until 4th or 5th grade.

Funny NOW Story: I had a friend who said that at the end of her 4th grade year her family moved to a new school district. Her previous school's scope & sequence taught states and capitals in the 5th grade, but her new school taught states and capitals in the 4th grade. So, she never learned about states and capitals. To put your mind at ease, she still turned out to be a fine adult and a good mother.

I got a lesson in how Scope and Sequence can be a hindrance for home education. Remember those world geography games on the computer? Well, my older children were having so much fun learning on the computer that my then four-year-old CHILD 6 started begging to play the games too. In my mind, he was not old enough because I remember learning about states and capitals in the 4th grade. Finally, I agreed to let this four-year-old play on the states and capitals section of the computer games. I thought, "What can it hurt?" and it will keep him busy. In about two to three weeks, he could move every state into place on a map and he knew all the names of the states and capitals. I was astounded and asked myself how this was possible. Then I realized how much better it was that he could learn at the time, place and pace that was best for him. By watching others learn and have fun, it gave him a desire to have fun and learn when he was ready and not at the pace of a Scope & Sequence.

Myth 38: *Every child needs their own grade level appropriate Science and Social Studies*

TRUTH: It works very well to teach all the different age-level children together at the same time on the same subject, especially in science and social studies. This is called "age integrated education."

I realized it was much easier and effective to do

what Jessica Hulcy calls "teach to the oldest child". This means if the oldest child is studying something in science and social studies, then all the children will be on the same topic.

Here's an example: The oldest student is taking Biology for high school which covers plants, animals, and people. So, younger children can be learning about plants, animals, and people right along with the older student. I love the family unity this provides since you can read together, watch videos together, do experiments together, and go on field trips together. Also, the verbal discussion that would go on between the children about what is being studied meant that the retention of information was heading toward 90%.

This made home education so much easier on me as well. I only had to make plans to cover one topic for science or social studies and I could teach all the children together like my own one room schoolhouse.

Note: Our children would have their own math and phonics/English program that was appropriate for their level. Two of my children were twenty months apart and I was able to teach them both math and English together because they were on similar levels of learning at that time.

Myth 39: *We need spelling books to learn to spell.*

TRUTH: Spelling can be made simple and inexpensive.

When we started schooling at home, we had spelling books with lists of words and activities for each week of school. My frustration was that we were spending a lot of money on these spelling books, which also took up a lot of our time. Many times, my children were reviewing words that they already knew.

Eventually, I found this efficient curriculum called *Natural Speller* by Kathryn Stout. I had heard Kathryn speak at a homeschool event, and I was inspired by her view of education. This spelling curriculum was inexpensive and was not consumable, meaning that I could use it for multiple children. Kathryn Stout gives lists of all the words a student needs to know for each grade level, 1st - 8th grade. Then for high school, she included an etymology section.

To use the ***Natural Speller*** curriculum (See Resources), I made a copy of the 1st -8th grade spelling word lists for each one of my children. Then, as I had time, I would call out a word. If my child could spell it and use it in a sentence, I took a bright yellow highlighter and I highlighted it off the child's spelling list. When I got to those words that the child didn't know, they would write it down and we would see how many times we could use that word during the next week.

Spelling doesn't come easy to everyone! If one of my children became discouraged, I would remind them of all the progress they had made. I would show them those highlighted words that they had learned and assure them that they could learn these other ones too. It's positive reinforcement.

It was probably a bizarre way to do spelling by some people's standards, but for us it was really successful. They could see how many words they knew, even though they might have some that would always be difficult. One of my children probably graduated still confused with the spelling of "which" and "witch." But, bless her heart, she knows a ton of other words. Again, being able to adapt the curriculum to the student's ability is one of the benefits of a one-on-one tutorial education that homeschooling allows.

REMEMBER: Today there are many spelling games on the computer, and there are many other fun ways to learn to spell as well.

Myth 40: *Education is all about reading books.*

TRUTH: Education is about retaining information, which can be accomplished in varying ways and is best done while having fun.

Why do traditional school parents tend to think that the most important thing we need to do is read and that reading is the only way to learn? Reading is important, but as a part of obtaining information for what's being learned experientially and to spark interest in more things to learn. We used books to learn some things that led to fun activities or field trips. Many times, if we were doing a hands-on project, it would lead us back to the books to find more information.

Years ago, I saw a little cartoon that was kind of sad in a way. The two characters were outside playing, and they saw a snake. One of them asked the other "What kind of snake is that?" and the other said, "I don't know, but we could go and look it up in a book." The response was, "No, that's too much like school."

We don't want our kids to think about education like that. We want our children to go look up information, figure out what something is, and learn more about the thing they saw or experienced in the real world. Helping our children to think and solve problems with both books and hands-on-experiences is vital.

A very wise veteran homeschool mom says:

"THIS IS HOW YOU HOMESCHOOL YOUR KIDS.
YOU PLAY, PLAY, PLAY, PLAY.
GIVE ME A LITTLE WORK.
GIVE ME A LITTLE BREAK
AND READ SOME BOOKS.
DO SOME MATH.
PLAY, PLAY, PLAY, PLAY, PLAY
READ SOME BOOKS, DO SOME MATH,
PLAY, PLAY, PLAY, PLAY, PLAY.
GRADUATE THEM"

— LANI CAREY

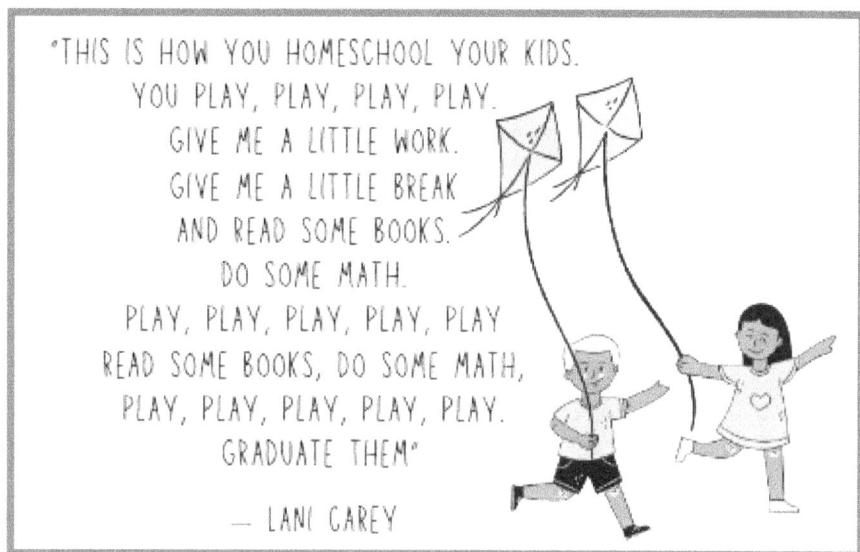

As homeschoolers we did a lot of "play," which included hands-on, audiovisual resources, demonstrations, field trips, games, experiments, building things, and taking things apart. Somebody might walk into all of this play and experiential learning and say, what is this teacher doing? In reality, we were learning motor skills, organizational skills, mental processing skills, cooperation, creativity, problem solving and so much more.

We turned cleaning the house into a learning and playing opportunity. When our house would get messy, I would tell my kids, "We're going to have organizational skills day." Then we would make a game out of cleaning up our house. There are a lot of skills that can be learned while cleaning, such as number concepts, classification, cooperation, language development, story development, comprehension, hand-eye coordination, mental health, problem solving, and much more. Following instructions was one of the biggest skills learned in this process.

These children are just playing.

Funny NOW Story: During the activities of the day, things seemed to be drawn like a magnet to every flat surface: floors, tables, and countertops. So about 30 minutes to an hour before my husband was going to be home, we would do a "sweep cleaning". I would get my broom, dustpan, trash can, and a laundry basket. Along with the children, I would go to each room. As I began by sweeping everything on the floor to the middle of the room, the children quickly claimed anything that was theirs. If it ended up in my basket it was mine and they would have to earn it back. This is called *motivation*. Then I would sweep up the dirt, put it in the trash can, and we would move to the next room. If we went to the next room and there was something in the basket that belonged there, we would put it away. By the time daddy came home we could at least see the floors and most flat surfaces.

However, I did end up with a basket of things that needed to find their homes again. This is when I provided another motivational tool. We did not watch much television and there weren't all the electronic distractions like there are available today; watching a movie on Friday night using a VHS tape was a big deal. VHS tapes don't have commercial breaks, but I decided to create my own. At a really suspenseful part of the movie, I would click pause on the remote and call "Clutter drill!" and the number of items they would need to each pick up before the movie would begin again. I gauged the number by how many things were in the clutter basket and how much needed to be picked up before bedtime. This way, when the movie was over, the house was fairly tidy. My house was never immaculate like my mom's. However, bringing play into every aspect of learning was and is so effective.

CHAPTER 6

Myths About Socialization

Myth 41: *Children need to be socialized in a traditional school environment.*

TRUTH: Homeschooling provides opportunities to socialize and to be prepared for adult socialization.

One of the most asked questions I got when someone found out we homeschooled our children was, "How will your child be socialized without going to school?" When I began homeschooling, I was very unsure about how to answer that question as it seemed to be questioning my choice to homeschool. Now I can say with confidence that homeschooling presents great opportunities for socialization on multiple levels, and I have grown to love answering the question about "socialization."

God provided again with a cassette tape series done by Gregg Harris, who worked to launch the Christian homeschooling movement in the 1980s and early 90s. In his talk, he discussed age-integrated socialization versus age-segregated socialization. From that talk, I developed a response to the socialization question:

"Are you talking about age-segregated socialization

135

or age-integrated socialization? In age-segregated socialization, students are divided up by age groups with no one older to lend their wisdom and no one younger to learn to serve. I have personally never worked anywhere that everyone was my same age; so, I am not sure how that prepares students for adulthood. In public-school socialization, students tend to learn things like cursing, smoking, drinking, drugs, peer pressure, bullying (today I would add gender confusion and test anxiety).

"Our family has chosen the age-integrated socialization method, which we find not only in our family interactions at home, but also at church, homeschool group events, community sports, and many other places. We can oversee that our children are learning well-rounded socialization skills like how to rock a baby in the church nursery, how to push a wheelchair at a nursing home, and how to look adults in the eyes. We can be there to teach our children that socialization involves showing respect and serving others.

"How much socialization is really happening in the traditional system? Consider that in traditional schools' students are constantly being told to sit down and be quiet."

By this point the person's eyes were glazed over and would just respond. "Okay".

There is a lot to process about the truth of socialization and there is a lot of research to back it up. I encourage you to stop and take some time to ponder the truth about socialization.

Myth 42: *Children will be unsocialized because they stay home all the time.*

TRUTH: Homeschool students have many opportunities to be involved in activities outside the home.

Another big comment about socialization was, "Your child won't get to go to the prom."

Funny NOW Story: I first heard this comment when CHILD 1 was 5 years old. I can tell you that at the time the prom was the least of my concerns. My reply was that many of my high school classmates did not go to the prom, and they turned out just fine as adults. When I look back and think about how much pressure was put on us to have a date for the prom in high school, I am not sure that was good socialization. It was like one's self-worth was based on whether you had a date to the prom. What went on at the prom wasn't entirely wholesome either. Not all socialization is good socialization.

The irony of the prom question is that our children all had the opportunity to get dressed up and attend some kind of formal dance. Some were invited to high school proms by a student from the high school. Others went to homeschool-sponsored formal dances. Homeschooling has grown so much in recent years that many homeschool groups put on their own formal dance events.

Socialization happens in families, at home, at church, at the grocery store, or at a park. But also, homeschool events, community sports, co-op, and tutorial opportunities are growing every day. I reached a point where I was ready to "anti-socialize" my children to get some rest. Our children had so many opportunities to socialize with other people that I had to pick and choose how much outside socialization to allow and still have time at home.

REMEMBER: Just like education happens everywhere, socialization is happening everywhere, too.

CHAPTER 7

Myths About Traditional School

Myth 43: *You must have a schedule like public school because they are the professionals.*

TRUTH: As a homeschool family, your daily schedule can be whatever works best for your family.

I want to describe what the schedule for my first few years of homeschooling looked like. We got up at 7:00 a.m. Everyone was dressed, fed and ready for school by 8:00 a.m. We did math at 8:00 a.m., English at 9:00 a.m., Science at 10:00 a.m., and Social Studies at 11:00 a.m. I'm pretty sure I rang a bell in between each class, and we said the Pledge of Allegiance. I am analytical and I like to plan. Benjamin Franklin said, "If you fail to plan, you plan to fail."

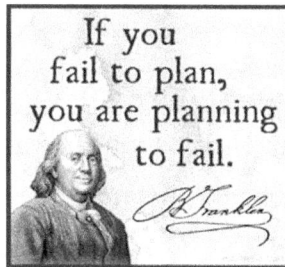

Funny NOW Story: I had a big poster on the wall with our well-defined school schedule. However, reality struck one day when a sweet lady from our church dropped by and saw my chart on the wall.

CLASS SCHEDULE

7 AM Get Up / Get Ready / Eat Breakfast
8 AM - Pledge of Allegiance to American Flag
          MATH
9 AM - ENGLISH
10 AM - SCIENCE
11 AM - SOCIAL STUDIES
  *** Ring Bell Between Classes
12 PM - LUNCH
1 PM - Finish work / Read Together
  *** RECESS
3 PM - CEAN UP
5 PM - DINNER
7 PM - FAMILY DEVOTIONS

She commented how wonderful it was that I was so organized. By that time, I had a new baby and a toddler whose needs never lined up with my well laid plan. I honestly admitted to my church friend that the chart on the wall was MY FANTASY of what a school day might look like. I had never had a school day that worked out exactly like that schedule.

Somehow, my children were still learning to read, write and do math without a perfect schedule that looked like traditional school. I learned to work school around our family life.

Myth 44: *You must do every subject 5 days a week because "normal" kids go to school 5 days a week.*

TRUTH: When you educate at home, you can set your schedule of how and when to teach different subjects.

You can organize your school week, month, or year to fit your child's learning style and your family's schedule. I decided that educating our children needed to revolve around our lives instead of having our lives revolve around school. Flexibility in scheduling allowed us to have time for field trips, community service, learning life skills and many other valuable life lessons. For our family, we typically only planned workbook instruction 3 - 4 days a week.

At least one day a week was connecting with other families during co-op. A lot of time during the week was spent working on projects or assignments needed for their weekly gathering with other homeschoolers. As our children got older and had jobs during the day, we created a flexible schedule so they could do one subject a day each

141

day of the week when they got home from work. This helped them develop time management skills. As long as they completed the work I had assigned to them, they could keep working their jobs.

I have worked with some students that did much better if they had no more than two or three core subjects going at a time. So, the student might do English and Social Studies in the fall and Science with Health in the spring. Math would be done all school year because it typically needs more repetition and practice.

Funny SUCCESS Story: I worked with a young man years ago who was failing and getting into trouble in public school. After talking with him, I suggested that he use a computer-based curriculum that would keep track of his schoolwork because his mom had to focus on her job. He would only focus on ONE core subject until it was completed. This usually took about 6-8 weeks. He went from failing to making A's and B's. He was encouraged to succeed in his education because of this unique opportunity. That being said, computer-based education with all the subjects in the same format is definitely not the best option for most students. However, in this young man's life, it was so much better than the pressures of public school and he was very successful.

These are just a few of the scheduling variations available to a homeschooling family. This is your home-school, and you can schedule education around your life.

Myth 45: *I must keep records to prove 180 days of attendance.*

TRUTH: **Homeschool parents educate their child 365 days a year, which far exceeds the 180 days of traditional school. Every day is a school day when you homeschool.**

I know parents with full spreadsheets of not only days, but every activity accomplished each day and the hours they did "school". With a family of six children there was no way I had time to sit down and just check off days, much less document what each child did. It would have taken away time needed to educate my children and take care of my family. Plus, I had a hard time differentiating between school and life. I realized we homeschooled 365 days a year from the minute our children's feet hit the floor to the minute they went to bed. And, sometimes, we used books. But everything we did could be a learning moment. We never missed an opportunity to master a concept or skill.

Funny NOW Story: When our oldest was five years old, he asked me what a car wreck was. I explained the best I knew how. A couple of weeks later, my two oldest children and I were in a terrible car accident, and we were trapped in our car. My first reaction was to turn around and tell my son, "This is a car wreck, and it is not good." Praise God! We all survived. Every moment is a teachable moment. Determining when to make it a teachable moment can take some learning for yourself.

Myth 46: *Students should be able to sit still and pay attention for 45-55 minutes of a class period.*

TRUTH: Attention spans vary between children, and they vary depending on the activity being done.

It has been determined that children have about one minute of attention for each year they have been alive, and then the activity needs to change to reset the attention span. I believe many struggles in learning may be prevented when breaks are given.

If I realized my child was getting fidgety, I had activities in mind like running upstairs, putting away their clean clothes, bringing down their dirty clothes, running around the house (one lap for each year of their life), and jumping on the trampoline fifty times. Go feed a pet. Sweep the porch. The list went on and on. A lot of household tasks could be completed in short, welcome breaks. And when the child returned, they were ready to work for another few minutes. However, if we were doing something very interesting and hands-on, there may be no need for a break at all.

Even as adults, many of us struggle with staying focused for very long if what is going on is mundane. I have learned that, even with a good speaker, I can pay more attention if I am taking notes or chewing gum.

REMEMBER: Understanding how short a child's attention span is can really help parents be more patient and can decrease a lot of frustration.

Myth 47: *School is a safe place.*

TRUTH: By and large, a home education environment will provide a safer, relaxed, less stressful place to learn.

I have been blessed to work as an academic counselor for homeschoolers. I love that I get the opportunity to work with families from all over the country. But I have been shocked at the stories I hear of why parents have decided to join the home education movement.

I noticed an increasing number of stories about students suffering with anxiety and depression to the point of needing professional help, and too often being admitted to mental health facilities. I came across research that associated the students being given computers for their education with this increased anxiety. How, you might ask, would this affect mental health? God created us to interact with other human beings as an emotional need. In the last decade and a half, more and more families spend most of their awake hours on some kind of electronic device. Much of the day is spent on the computer at school, and then many children come home to parents who are addicted to their own phones, TV, and other electronic devices. Many times, electronics are the babysitter… but at what cost? How many times have you been to a restaurant and the whole family is looking at their phones and not talking?

I want to scream, "Wake up parents! You will only have the children under your roof for a short time. When they are gone, you will realize how much time you wasted that you could have spent with your children."

Also, parents don't seem to realize that human interaction fulfills a vital human need just as much as food, clothing, and a roof over their heads provides.

Now the reasons for the exodus from traditional schools have only worsened. In public schools, teachers, principals and even school resource officers have been stripped of the authority to maintain order and to give consequences or take action against students' inappropriate behavior.

Students' rights to feel good about themselves seems to be outweighing the safety and sanity of the other students and the school staff. The reality is that a world with no boundaries is chaotic, and most students don't feel safe. I think it has been a root cause of the high rate of anxiety, depression, drug usage, and suicide that is growing every day among the young. It is well known that most school shooters have been unhappy, anxious, drug users or just didn't feel like they fit in, to the point where they acted out their frustration.

Funny NEVER Story: I had homeschooling parents come talk to me at a convention. They began to explain how their 9th grade son had begged them to go to the local high school. The parents told their son that if he went, he would need to stick it out the whole year. None of them knew what this young man would face. Within a short time, their son was being advanced upon for sexual acts by other boys. When he would not consent, he was harassed cruelly. This cruelty advanced into death threats and knives were pulled on him at school. This young man got scared enough to tell his parents that he didn't want to live if he had to finish out the school year. When his parents heard this, they immediately removed their son from public school. The parents totally underestimated what expecting their son to stick to a decision was costing him and their family. Thankfully, they changed course.

I tell parents to first think long and hard about whether there is any way to avoid putting their child in a potentially unsafe situation. I also tell parents to always give their child the option to come home.

It's hard to imagine that sometimes abuse comes from teachers and administrators, too. Other times they may just look the other way and ignore what is happening.

Many teachers and administrators are trying the best they can to educate the children entrusted to their care. I can only imagine the pressure and frustration these teachers and administrators must be under to bravely go into what may seem to be impossible situations.

Another concern to be aware of is that with so many students moving from traditional schools to homeschooling, many of the safety issues need to be considered in homeschool groups as well. Some families also come openly wanting secular options. Please choose carefully any tutorials, co-ops, and groups to be sure they align with your family values.

I was talking to one co-op group leader who said they do not open enrollment to just anyone. Their families can only join on the recommendation of another family in good standing. One tutorial I am aware of requires families to homeschool at least one year before enrollment will be considered. Numerous new co-ops and tutorials have started since 2020 and many are wonderful. **No matter what path you choose for your student's education, BE INVOLVED. Don't acquiesce oversight of your student's education to someone else.**

CHAPTER 8

Myths About Struggling Learners

Myth 48: *My child should be held back because they can't read on grade level.*

TRUTH: Determine your child's grade level by their appropriate age for that grade and teach them according to their ability.

I hear statements like, "Children should be held back because they aren't on grade level." It makes me want to ask for a reality check on how that will play out in adult life. With this myth, I questioned what determines the grade level. If you could walk into any traditional school classroom you would find students with different reading abilities. I realized that one subject should not determine the grade level in homeschooling. At home, we can adapt what and how things are taught to the individual child. Then we can put the child in an age-appropriate grade level and teach to their ability.

Funny NOW Story: If you meet a homeschooler and ask what grade they are in, they may not know. They may be using a 3rd grade math book and a 5th grade language arts program but are in the 4th grade class at church. In this situation, I suggest parents can instruct their child to say they are in the 4th grade if anyone should ask.

Reading is just one facet of Language Arts, so let's talk about Language Arts. Language Arts seems to be all about reading and writing, but it is really about teaching students how to communicate. Language Arts is the art of language. We think that in order to write, students typically need to know grammar and spelling, and that may look different for children who have different capabilities.

Funny NOW Story: Our family moved to Ashland, Ohio in 1993 so my husband could go to seminary. Our neighbors next door, Greg and Sharon, were seminary students as well. Greg, who was extremely intelligent, walked with a limp. As we became friends, Sharon shared that Greg had had polio as a child and that when he was in public school, he could not read, write, or do math. He was labeled as retarded, stupid, and unable to learn. When Sharon met Greg, she saw something very different in him and began to read books to him. Greg could memorize anything he heard. Sharon took the time to discover how Greg learned. He decided to go to college. With his precious wife by his side, reading his required books and typing the papers he dictated to her, Greg earned his bachelor's degree. By the time we met him, he was not far from getting his master's degree. What is interesting is that it was only in adulthood that Greg was diagnosed with dyslexia.

Dyslexia is common to many brilliant people who simply need to learn a different way. World changers like Thomas Edison, Albert Einstein, Henry Ford, the Wright Brothers, Wolfgang Mozart, George Washington, and many more were dyslexic.

While living in Ohio, we visited the birthplace of Thomas Edison more than once. I loved to hear the story of how Thomas Edison was sent home from the local school with a note that basically said that he was unteachable and would not amount to anything. The story was that Thomas Edison's mom tucked that note in her apron pocket and told young Edison that the school didn't know how to teach him. She homeschooled Edison, and the results amaze us today.

When determining your child's grade level, put your student on the grade level that is age appropriate for going to church or some other activity that is appropriate for other children your child's age. Then teach them on whatever level is appropriate for reading and math.

Myth 49: *My child is struggling with reading, so we are stopping his other activities to focus entirely on reading.*

TRUTH: Focusing on the weakness will only tend to make a student feel defeated and worthless. Focus and shine the spotlight on the giftings of a child.

Focusing on or pointing out where students struggle can be very discouraging and can hinder the learning process. I hear stories of students in traditional school being denied recess or art class because they are not performing well academically. Many times, recess, art, or breaks are what is needed to allow the student to refocus.

Put the spotlight on something the student is good at doing. Incorporate reading together about topics the student shows an interest in. Give frequent breaks to allow time to refocus. Be willing to find out if there are any other challenges like dyslexia or if there is a need for glasses that could be hindering the reading.

We had six different learning styles in our house, but I started watching for the interests and giftings in each of my children. Seeing the different learning styles made me realize I would need to use their interests and giftings to provide the opportunity to showcase what they had learned.

For my oldest son, reading and math seemed to come easy. But if you wanted him to draw, color, or sing, that was another story. My fifth child was dyslexic; reading and math did not come easy for her. But she loved to draw, had a keen understanding of color, and she sang very well. If I had waited until she could read well to let her draw, color, or sing, she would have been a frustrated and discouraged child.

I tried not to compare my children to each other or any other person's child because I knew God creates everybody differently. It can be a hard task to not compare ourselves to others, to look down on people who can't do what we can, or to feel belittled by others' accomplishments. I am convinced that if we look for the special purpose and giftings God has placed in our children, we will find them. As they build their confidence in other areas besides reading, there is no telling what they will be able to do.

Myth 50: *All children must read early or they are not smart.*

TRUTH: Students read when their brain is ready for them to read. Some students will need audiovisual help with reading. Obtaining the information is what matters.

It's OK. Really, it is. It really doesn't matter exactly when they learn to read.

Funny NOW Story: The first experience I had with this myth was with a dear friend of mine who decided to homeschool because her first-grade son, who did well in math and science in public school, was being held back because of his reading skills. My friend wasn't having anything to do with that. She knew her son would read when he was ready. While he did learn to read a little later than "normal", today he owns his own business and provides well for his family. I am pretty sure no one cared when he started reading.

Another Funny NOW Story: In my own family, I noticed early on that our very sweet 5th child had some struggles with traditional approaches to reading, writing and math. She tried so hard and had a wonderful attitude, but even in 4th grade she was still sounding out small words and not reading fast enough to remember what she read. We had a precious gentleman from our church that came over two to three days a week to help with her reading, but she still struggled.

When we decided to move to a new state, God provided refurbished laptop computers for my younger 3 children. So, I decided to give *Switched on Schoolhouse* a try. I knew we would be moving too late in the school year to start a co-op when we arrived, and I thought it would be easier for them and me to keep up with their schoolwork. It probably would have been okay for just Math and English, but all 4 core subjects in the same format became quite mundane and boring after years of hands-on-learning.

One great thing came out of that experience. Our dyslexic child figured out that she could highlight the text on the screen and have the computer read it out loud to her. The program was designed so that the word that was being read was highlighted and would move at a regular reading speed. Before long, I noticed a significant difference in her reading ability. I realized she had made a connection in her brain by being able to hear and see the words at the same time. I also learned that she was an audiovisual learner. Learning that she is an audiovisual learner changed the approach I used to teach her and lines up with the statistics that students retain more information if they do audiovisual learning. She went on to become an honor student in college.

Many parents who patiently waited for their child to learn to read have told me that once their child began to read, they loved reading. Be patient and allow your child to read in their own time.

Myth 51: *Parents need expensive reading programs to teach their children to read.*

TRUTH: Teaching a child to read can be inexpensive, but it does require an investment of your time. This is a time that can be a treasured memory as you teach each child at their own pace and on a path filled with a lot of enthusiastic praise.

Remember the statistic that most children don't have a long attention span and you can expect their attention to be about one minute for every year they have been alive. This became very real to me with my Energizer Bunny boy. You may have one at your house, too. It is the child that's all over the place and into everything. I wondered how I would get this child to sit still long enough to learn to read. I knew I had 5 minutes or less each day to teach him to read.

Funny SUCCESS Story: I found a great phonics book called *Teach Your Child to Read in 100 Easy Lessons*. I was excited because I knew the lessons were short and I could teach to mastery. However, when I showed my son the book, he was not thrilled at all and kept looking to see where the end of the book was and not paying much attention to what I was trying to show him. I realized that the big book was overwhelming, and he was trying to figure out how he could conquer it. I decided to do something unorthodox. I took the book to a bookbinder, had him cut the binding off the book and bore holes in it so the book would fit in a big three ring binder.

I would only take 2-3 pages out of the binder each day and then he felt like he conquered those pages. He felt successful, rather than just having a big book to conquer. Even though this was out-of-the-box, I didn't have to feel like I had to keep the book intact. If breaking the book down is what it took to make it easier for my son to learn to read, I am glad to have done it. Since then, I've taught several people, from children to adults, to read using this very simple method.

There was another way I could get double benefits. I would enthusiastically tell my husband about our son's accomplishments. Then I would have our son show off for his dad by reviewing the day's lesson.

You don't have to spend a lot of money to teach your kids to read. It's really not hard. It's just using some simple things, but it does take dedication. Some kids might catch on really fast, but others may need to have a bit more time. With this particular child, I just set my goal that if he reads by the time he is nine, I'm going to count it a good job. With this teaching method, he was reading pretty well by the age of 6 or 7. It just depends on that particular child as to what they're able to do. Some of my kids were reading a lot earlier than that, but I really can't compare because they all can read as adults.

That said – There are curricula and programs designed to help with specific learning challenges like dyslexia. You may need additional resources to assist you. I would encourage you to seek out someone who has experience with these options to help you figure out what might work well for your child. Two resources I know of are *Inspiring Minds* and *Homeschooling with Dyslexia*.

The investment of your time and patience in encouraging your child's reading success can't be measured in money. It is measured in the memories and joy of time spent together.

Myth 52: *Students have to memorize math facts in order to do higher level math. No calculators are allowed.*

TRUTH: A calculator is a wonderful kinesthetic tool for math when a student isn't able to memorize math facts.

Let's look at math myths. What are the basics of math? The basics of math are addition, subtraction, multiplication, division, fractions, decimals and percents. How much math do we really need to know to be successful in life?

Funny NOW Story: I was that geeky math kid in school. I

did all the high school level math so well that when I got to my senior year, the guidance counselor suggested I become an accountant. I did become an accountant, and the only math I use is addition, subtraction, multiplication, division, fractions, decimals and percents, and I use a calculator. I never used any of that high level math I had learned in high school for my job.

Funny NOW Story: Basic math concepts are important. However, I work with many students, including one of my girls, that just could not memorize math facts no matter how much she tried. But she understood the math concepts. If I asked her for the answer to 8 X 5, she could not automatically say 40, but on her fingers could count 5, 10, 15, 20, 25, 30, 35, 40. This meant she understood the concept. I realized that she needed a kinesthetic tool called a calculator.

By high school, a calculator is an acceptable tool for math. It provides a way to go on to higher level math, bypassing the need to memorize math facts.

Every time a person enters a problem in a calculator, it also works like a flash card. The repetition of entering the math problems can help students master those facts. Allowing a child to use a calculator may help that child to excel beyond what they think is possible. Being able to successfully progress in math will boost their confidence.

CHAPTER 9

Myths About High School, College and Careers

I want to preface this final chapter concerning myths about high school, college, and careers to explain that many of the previous myths apply here as well, but some of the **MYTHS** here have kept parents from continuing homeschooling through high school. In this chapter, I want to discuss **TRUTHS** that empower parents to homeschool their high schoolers.

Myth 53: *If I don't get high school perfectly right, I will ruin my child's life.*

TRUTH: There is no perfect way to homeschool high school. The only way to get it "right" is to do what is best for your student to fulfill the credit requirements needed to graduate and to help your student be prepared for adulthood.

I realized that the scariest time of homeschooling is most likely when parents start thinking about high school. We are led to believe that if we as parents don't get it right or perfect, that we could ruin our child's lives, or at least their chances for a successful future.

I am not sure why I was not really intimidated by high school, but I can assure you I did not know much about what I was doing. There really wasn't anyone I could turn to ask questions. However, when I did have questions, God's faithfulness to bring answers was just as real as any other time in my journey.

I realized there was more than one way to earn the needed credits, and meeting graduation requirements was not nearly as hard as I had thought. The key to freedom from this myth was allowing each child's high school experience to be unique and to prepare them for their future.

Today, there are many tools and resources to help you, and there are many who have walked this journey before you as well. I love to help families find their freedom to enjoy the journey through high school.

<u>ENGLISH</u> - Let me start out by saying that each year of high school English should include a literature and composition component, and there are definitely MYTHS related to these components.

Myth 54: *The only way to cover literature is to READ the actual books or a literature textbook.*

TRUTH: Literature can be covered by using books, audiobooks, and movies.

When I went to high school, students were expected to read books because we did not have audiobooks or movies available. What I found strange is that we weren't even allowed to read Cliff Notes if we were totally uninterested in reading the book. However, times have changed, and many pieces of literature are now available in audiobooks and have been made into movies. I would happily let my children read the summary of the book to at least be aware of the content. I am not trying to say, reading isn't wonderful; but if you think about it, most of us would rather read what we want to read instead of reading what is required of us.

Funny NOW Story: Child 5, if you remember, has dyslexia. As an adult, she explained that she thought the words on a page jumped around for everyone. Can you imagine trying to read with the words moving around? When she got to high school, I just knew that reading literature was not an option for her. This was when I found out about a high school curriculum called *Movies as Literature* by Kathryn Stout. It opened a whole new understanding of literature for all of us. I say 'us' because I learned more about English literature than I had ever learned before. We would pop popcorn or get a pizza and have Friday movie nights. Over the course of the first year we covered 17 movies, and instead of writing in the workbook, we would have a family discussion about the questions from the workbook. The second year, we looked up movies that came from British literature and continued Kathryn's style of teaching literature. Did you know that *Chitty, Chitty Bang, Bang*, *Mary Poppins*, *101 Dalmatians*, *Sherlock Holmes*, and so many more came from British literature. I always wondered why Walt Disney gave the actors British accents. In two years, we learned about forty pieces of literature. I am not sure I could have told you about four pieces of literature when I graduated from high school. There are no maximum or minimum pieces of literature you must cover. Even a recommended book list is up to your discretion, but you can still use audiobooks and movies.

One of our daughters loved audiobooks and still loves to listen to books. Another son was watching one of the movies and realized that there was a trilogy book series and wanted to read the books. Using movies and audiobooks actually sparked their interest in learning even more about literature.

You could go on to do American literature as movies, world literature as movies, children's literature as movies, Christian literature as movies, and so many more to fulfill the English credits for high school graduation.

There are now other resources available that can assist with generating ideas for using audiovisual aids for literature.

Even if you are using a curriculum that recommends you read a book, you have the freedom to choose whether to read the book, listen to an audiobook, or watch a movie. You can even do all three. This is your homeschool and you are free to do what works for your student.

Myth 55: *Composition is about having good handwriting, grammar, and spelling. They will need these skills to go to college.*

TRUTH: Composition is about getting thoughts out of the mind and onto a piece of paper.

Let me start this explanation by sharing a revelation I had about composition. I always thought reading and writing went together, and if a student is good at one, they would naturally be good at the other. **REVELATION: A good reader does not necessarily like to write**.

Funny NOW Story: Child 1 was a speed reader from an early age, yet I have never seen anyone hate writing as much as he did. One day, I asked him to take one sheet of notebook paper, double space, and just write about whatever he wanted to write about, and he wrote something like this. *I hate to write. I really don't like to write. I wished I didn't have to write. I don't like my teacher because she makes me write. I really don't want to write. Please don't make me write.* I found this funny because what he wrote was creative writing. However, I did want to figure out what was causing his reluctance to write, especially since I hadn't particularly liked writing in school either.

In the beginning, when Child 1 first started to write, my reaction, when he was finished, was to immediately start critiquing it for grammar and spelling. I would circle and mark all the mistakes just like my public-school teacher had done. One day, this son who hated to write, looked at me and said, "You don't even read what I write. All you care about is grammar!" He was right. I was focused on the logistics of spelling and grammar because I didn't recognize there was a difference between spelling and grammar and the content of a paper. I then realized that if a person never becomes great at grammar and spelling, they can always have somebody correct that part. However, people can't get somebody else to think for them or to get their thoughts out of their head onto paper.

I began to look at the writing aspect of education in a different way, and again I wanted to do whatever it took to make learning work. With my oldest son, I learned that when he wrote something, I didn't have to look at it. I could simply have him read it back to me so he could hear what he had written. I figured if he couldn't read it to me, there was no chance that I would be able to read it. Many times he would correct himself or catch his own mistakes. In the middle of his reading he would say things like, "that was a long sentence", "that's not how that word is spelled", or "I should have capitalized that word." He might say, "that's not what I really meant to say." This unique technique took this particular child from being one who didn't like to write at all to getting A's on papers in college writing assignments. I think this only happened because I quit trying to cage him in with my traditional school expectations and, instead, I embraced his way of learning.

When we started using the *Movies as Literature* workbook, I realized that writing answers in the workbook wasn't helpful. However, using the questions from the workbook to initiate a discussion after the movie was over was an incredible way to get my teenagers talking. I realized having my teenager communicate verbally what she was thinking opened the door to getting ideas on paper. I would have the student write about their favorite character, scene, or something we talked about. I didn't tell them how much to write, but over time my students became more comfortable and proficient at writing more and more.

BONUS Funny Now Story: When Child 5 went to college

she mentioned how it seemed the students didn't know how to have a discussion in class without becoming offended, arguing with the professor, and being disrespectful. She believed that the Friday night movie discussions had prepared her to be good at classroom discussions and accepting of others' opinions. Many times, using these different approaches to learning reaped more benefits than I expected.

Myth 56: *My teenager must write neatly and tilt their letters the same way.*

TRUTH: Handwriting does not determine how smart you are, doesn't have to be neat, and is unique to each person.

Funny NOW Story: When I was young, teachers made a big deal of writing neatly, that it had to be the same height and spacing and tilted in the same direction. My handwriting was very neat, but I didn't tilt my letters like the teacher wanted, which was unacceptable. My twin brother was left-handed, and the teachers wanted to make him write with his right hand. I guess the fruit doesn't fall far from the tree because my mom wasn't putting up with this and advocated for my brother to be able to write how it came naturally to him.

Let's talk about handwriting:

As I mentioned before, each year of high school English should contain both a literature and composition component. Many times, we confuse handwriting with composition. It is important to separate the two. When students are young, they begin to develop the art of handwriting, but fine motor skills develop at different ages and can be different for boys and girls. You will find that some children catch on quickly and write beautifully, while others don't write so well because their fine motor skills and hand-to-eye coordination are not fully developed yet.

An interesting observation I made through the years was the handwriting of male students and even some girls. Boys who might write fairly well in their younger years often became messy writers after puberty. My boys wrote neatly all through their younger grades. Then they got to the age where they matured, and their bodies were changing. Suddenly, they started writing just like their father, which isn't terrible, but it wasn't like I had taught them to write. My husband did not teach them to write so the change wasn't because they were copying his writing. I also noticed that two of my three girls' handwriting was like mine. But our middle daughter realized her handwriting looked more like her grandfather's handwriting. It would be interesting to know if there are statistics on a genetic connection to handwriting.

I have talked to many parents of boys. Very few say their boy's handwriting is neat after a certain point in development. I began to see this repeatedly to the point that I just tell parents to not freak out over handwriting. It is not because that young man is deliberately being messy, sloppy, or lazy. Being upset and angry over it is not going to make that student have any better handwriting.

There is another factor that may affect the handwriting change at this stage is brain development. It could be that the brain is running faster than the hand can write what the student is thinking.

My oldest brother was considered a genius. I remember as a young child being told that he was being allowed to learn to type in 4th and 5th grade because the teachers knew he was smart, but they couldn't read anything he wrote.

Our Child 1 was so much like this that I would let him record what he wanted to write into a tape recorder. Then he could listen, write it down, and read it to me.

When I was growing up, people found it funny that doctors are usually extremely book smart, but you can't read their handwriting on a prescription. Think about this when you want to fuss about handwriting.

REMEMBER: Handwriting is an art and not everyone is good at art, and it definitely looks different for each person.

Myth 57: *You must have a separate curriculum for each credit of high school.*

TRUTH: A subject-integrated approach to learning allows you to use the same curriculum to cover several credits for high school at one time.

There are some high school unit study curricula that hook subjects together where students can earn 3 or more credits. One that our family used was *KONOS History of the World* by Jessica Hulcy. In this high school curriculum, students may earn several credits in history and geography, English literature and composition, Christian worldview, Bible, fine art, music, critical thinking, humanities, speech, and study skills.

Notgrass by Ray and Charlene Notgrass is another great unit study approach to high school where students may earn credits in English, history, and Bible using this one integrated method of education. Integrating subjects can also be done with curriculum like *BiblioPlan* by Rob and Julia Nalle and *The Mystery of History* by Linda Lacour Hobar. Many of these curricula also include timelines and hands-on activity ideas that help students put it all in perspective and give them a visual picture of history.

Using a subject-integrated approach for high school allows students to earn credits more easily than having to study each subject individually. Students retain more information when subjects are taught together. This simplifies the learning process and encourages the student because they can see their learning time accelerated.

Math and Science – If I wanted to offer classes in any subject that would guarantee I would have students, it would be math and science. Parents seem to be the most intimidated by these subjects; so, let me clarify some MYTHS and bring some TRUTHS to these two subjects.

Myth 58: *I have to hire someone to teach science because I can't do Labs.*

TRUTH: Anything hands on is a Lab and videos can count as labs too.

It's actually easy to do labs at home, because anything hands-on is a "lab." A lab is not just what is done in a laboratory or when you have a microscope, test tube, or Bunsen burner; many things count as labs.

Funny NOW Story: Shortly before our Child 1 was ready for high school, a group of homeschoolers took a field trip to a university science lab. I wish I knew who the professor was that gave the tour, but that tour changed my whole way of looking at science for high school.

While on the field trip, we were encouraged to ask questions, so I decided to ask what kind of microscope to get my son for high school science so he would be ready for college. (I assumed I needed one because I remembered having one in my high school science classes.) The professor's answer opened my eyes to a new way of getting my children prepared to love science.

He said, "Don't buy a microscope. Buy magnifying glasses. A magnifying glass will magnify as well as any microscope you can afford to buy, and your children will be able to magnify more things and maybe they will see that science is all around them. Maybe they will get excited enough about science to show up in my lab. Most kids think science is reading a book, taking a test, and they have no interest in pursuing science in college. Ma'am, get these kids excited about science. And if they show up in my lab, it will be easy to teach them about Bunsen burners, test tubes, and microscopes." From that point on I knew my job was to get my children excited about science.

When the professor mentioned that science is all around us, I began to apply that to my education plan. As a color blind woman who cannot tell when a plant is dead, I knew I needed some help in getting my children excited about plants. If I was teaching Biology and the children were studying plants, I would set up field trips to the plant

175

experts - an orchard, a greenhouse, a florist, or a nature science center. What better lab could there be than the real thing? I was determined to put my children in front of people who love plants, and it was so much fun.

My goal was to find people who loved and were passionate about whatever science we were studying. And what could be more of a lab than going to where people are using and dealing with the topics of science we were studying?

This worked great until I remembered that I had dissected frogs and worms in a high school biology lab. The only things I learned were that formaldehyde smells really bad and it was hard to see the parts inside the tiny creatures. Then I looked up the cost of buying something to dissect and there was no way I was going to spend that much money.

Then one day I was getting a chicken ready for dinner and pulled out that sack that comes in the middle. It dawned on me that this chicken had been alive and a much bigger animal than a frog and worm. I told the children to get their magnifying glasses out and we were going to have a lab. We looked at the skin tissue, fat tissue, fascia tissue, muscle tissue, bones, ligaments, gizzard, liver, heart and that wonderful neck. If you cut the neck open, you can see vertebrae and even look to see where it connected to the rest of the chicken before its demise. There is bone marrow and if you put a leg bone in a glass of coke for a few days, you may not have to buy soft drinks at your house anymore. This was such a fun, easy way to do a lab and then we cooked the chicken and had it for dinner.

One day my husband took the children fishing and when they came home with a string of fish, I spread a tarp over the picnic table and asked my husband to do an aquatic animal dissection and explanation while cleaning fish. The children would come running into the house, and show me the fish eggs they had found and tell me about how fish have babies.

When a child's eyes light up with excitement that is when real learning is happening. Most children who grow up on a farm live in a biology lab with gardens to grow plants that people eat, and animals that eat plants. Then people eat plants and animals. We learned how some animals' purpose is to serve people: cats catch mice, dogs protect and herd, horses are used for transportation and so forth. All of this is science with a lab.

Funny NOW Story: While teaching in a co-op in southern Michigan, the leaders had a problem finding anyone who would teach science to the K-6th graders. It so happened that year I was planning on teaching our 11th grader chemistry. I volunteered to teach chemistry to the K-6th graders with my daughter as my helper thus using their classes as her lab. The moms thought there was no way I could teach chemistry to K-6th graders. I was convinced I could teach them anything if I made it fun.

When I taught these chemistry classes, I looked up every experiment I could find that related chemistry to food. Most kids are interested in food. We started each class by singing the Atoms Family, which is a great YouTube video, done by a homeschool family, of course. The family is dressed like the Addams Family, and they made up a song describing atoms to the Addams Family tune. We built atoms and molecules out of various sizes and colors of marshmallows. They learned to read the periodic table and how the numbers on the periodic table are used to build the atom, and then how they form molecules. By the end of the semester, those students knew about gas, liquids, solids, atoms, molecules, mixture vs. chemical reaction, and the Periodic Table. They learned about diffusion by baking cookies and seeing how long it took for the smell to get to the rest of the co-op and kids to come looking for cookies.

These same fun things can be used for high school chemistry. I learned more teaching chemistry this way than I had learned in high school. I bet those kids were so excited to take chemistry in high school, which may have led them to pursue something chemistry related in college.

Today it's even easier to teach this way. There are chemistry courses that emphasize chemistry in cooking like Guest Hollow's <u>High School Chemistry in the Kitchen</u> or The Homeschool Scientist's <u>Culinary Science aka Kitchen Chemistry</u>.

REMEMBER: Science without a lab is really not science at all. Science labs are all around you in nature, your kitchen, the computer, YouTube videos, etc. Get excited with your children and engage creativity since the world is your classroom and your lab.

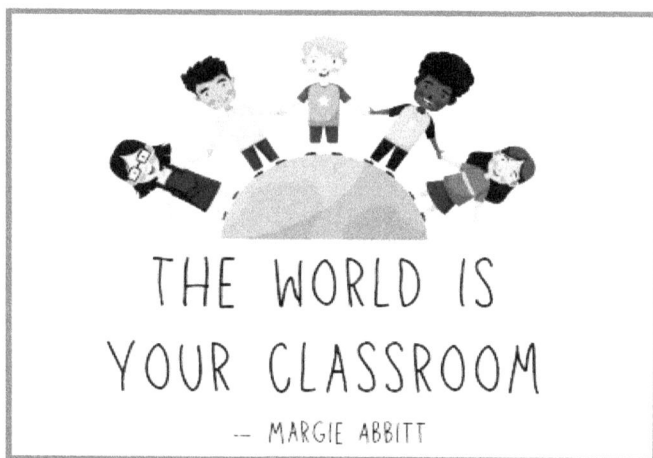

THE WORLD IS YOUR CLASSROOM
-- MARGIE ABBITT

Myth 59: *Students must have at least Algebra I, Geometry, and Algebra II to graduate and go to college.*

TRUTH: There are other options to meet the math requirements for college and careers.

I want to debunk the myth that every student must have higher levels of math to go to college or do well in life. It has been my experience that math requirements depend on the college the student plans to attend and what degree program that student will pursue. If a child is not strong in math, then there is a good chance God is not calling them into a field that requires strong math skills. I believe that which God calls you to do, He will prepare you to do.

The truth is many college degree programs may only require a College General Math (Basic Math) or College Algebra, or maybe only Statistics. This means you only need the math required for that degree program. Another truth is that many colleges will work with you to meet the math requirements. They offer placement tests, and if you don't place into college level math, they offer remedial math classes. If a student is college bound, always contact the college the student is interested in attending for exactly what math will be required under the degree program the student will be pursuing so the student doesn't find themselves taking courses they will never use.

You might also be surprised to find out that students don't need Algebra II to graduate from high school and go to college, but there are also other parts of the standard math curriculum in America that are useless. In addition, there are practical math skills needed in many real jobs that most students never get to in traditional school.

Remember: Focus on strengths not weaknesses and people are more likely to find their calling.

Funny NOW Story: I liked math in high school and did well. When I started homeschooling, I met parents worried about teaching math and I thought I could help by tutoring. The first thing I learned is that parents don't bring kids who like math to a math tutor, but these students consistently asked me the same question. You may have heard it at your house, too. "When will I ever use this?" I wanted to be able to explain this to them, but I had a hard time. My best explanation for most of Algebra 1 was that it would teach them good reasoning and problem-solving skills, but I did not find a lot of practical applications. In geometry, I did better in pointing out how geometry is used in practical ways. However, I really couldn't find any practicality in the proofs. In my whole adult life, no one had ever asked me about the theorem for mathematical equations. I recently had a high school math teacher tell me that she does not have to teach proofs anymore. Then Algebra 2 left me at a total loss as to when my students would use it.

Determined to find an answer, I asked my brothers, who are engineers in two different career fields, when they used Algebra 2 in their jobs. They both kind of chuckled and explained that Algebra 2 is a "logic math," not a practical math. Practical math is math that people use in real jobs. Being a very logical person, I could find no logic in spending a year teaching my students something that would have no practical use in real life.

I determined I would not teach or require Algebra 2 for my students, and many homeschoolers questioned this decision. It was like I was destroying my children's future. But I knew in my heart that if Algebra 2 was useless for real jobs, I shouldn't waste time on it.

REMEMBER: If you don't cover something in high school, it will be okay for them to learn that in college. With all that college costs, students should have to learn something in college.

Our children went on to do whatever they wanted, including attending college, joining the military, and developing careers, with no one questioning whether they had Algebra 2. In addition, the math skills needed for most college entrance exams like ACT/ SAT are those practical math skills my brothers talked about.

There is only one math program I have found that teaches practical high level math skills in the first four credits of the program: *Triad Math* by Craig Hane (a.k.a. Dr. Del). This program offers up to nine credits all the way to STEM engineering math for those who want a challenge. I know not everything works for every student, but this is definitely worth checking out.

The other thing that excited me about this program is that the first thing that Dr. Del does is teach the students how to use an inexpensive scientific calculator. I grew up in the "no calculator" generation and felt like I was cheating when I gave my students a calculator the night before the ACT. I had no knowledge that someone could teach them how to use all the keys on the calculator. I realized that for my students (mostly boys) that handwriting caused careless mistakes in math, but now they had a kinesthetic tool that would help increase their accuracy and speed whether taking the ACT test, taking a college course, or during their career.

Funny NOW Story: I found *Triad Math* because one of my adult sons realized he did not have the math he needed to pass a certification for his job. Within a couple of days, another homeschool mom asked my opinion on this curriculum, which I had never heard of before. What caught my attention was that Dr. Del mentioned something about finding himself tutoring college graduates in math that they should have learned in high school. I contacted *Triad Math* and I know they probably wondered what hit them when I came with all my questions. I desperately wanted to find an answer. *Triad Math* got my son started on their high school program, which allowed him to work at his own pace to master the concepts, testing out of what he already knew, and filling in the gaps of what he did not know. Within about 6 months or less, my son was testing out of every certification. At one point, he was offered a job on the spot based on the results of the math test given in the job interview.

BE AWARE: If the job requires any math skills, many companies are filtering out job applicants with math tests before offering the first interview. One of our daughters is a nurse. Even with a bachelor's degree, the hospital had her take a math test to make sure she had the basic math skills to be a nurse.

I encourage you to not waste your time during your high school years teaching math that your student will never use. Keep math as simple as possible in high school by finding the best way to teach the math your child needs for their future goals.

Myth 60: *Students must learn to write in a foreign language.*

TRUTH: Students will rarely need to write a foreign language, but they will always need to speak it.

When I realized that most high schoolers are

expected to learn a foreign language, I did like I had done with so many things and evaluated my experience. I'd had two years of Spanish in high school. I can currently speak about two or three sentences in Spanish and can count to ten. I believe that I could learn that much of any language in an afternoon. I began to talk to other parents and couldn't find anyone that was taught a foreign language in America that was bilingual, but every person I met from another country could speak at least two languages.

Once when I was at an event, I asked a lady what she did for a living. She said, "I teach people to speak bilingually." My immediate response was, "What are we doing wrong in America?" She immediately said, "It is taught backwards in America. You should always teach a child to speak a language before you teach them to write a language. If you think about it, you were speaking English at least 5 years before you went to school to learn to write it." She went on to say, "Your student will probably never need to write the language, but they will always need to speak it. It will be much easier to learn to write the language if you can already speak it."

I asked her what I was to do because there was no way I could immerse my children in a foreign language like the way I learned English. She suggested an app called *Duolingo*, and it was amazing how quickly our children learned to speak more Spanish than I had ever learned. Now there are so many great programs like *talkbox.mom*, *Babbel*, and *Mango Languages* to help your student actually learn to speak a foreign language.

Funny NOW Story: I was telling a college professor one time about this myth, and she told me that she was sure students needed to learn to write a foreign language to improve their grammar skills. All I could think is that English grammar is taught 3rd through 8th grade in traditional schools. If a student hadn't learned grammar, then how is forcing them to learn it in another language going to help?

Myth 61: *Homeschoolers will have a hard time getting accepted to and attending college.*

TRUTH: Homeschooled students are typically very successful in their ambitions for college, military, or whatever life pursuits they may have.

Because we did not homeschool in the box, I got asked questions like these: "How will your children ever go to college having so much fun?" or "How can your children possibly get a good education and learn everything they need to know without an intense curriculum and when they are out working a job during the school day?" I don't know why, but I was never concerned whether they would go to college or not. I think I knew deep inside that if I could teach them to love to learn, they would be able to learn for the rest of their lives. I do believe that it was

186

because we were very Non-Traditional that our children were successful with college.

A lot of people today use the word "unschooling" to describe learning in a non-traditional way. It is an old word with a new meaning. The original meaning was "uneducated, untaught, untrained, and undisciplined; not provided with school." The newer meaning behind that word "unschooling" is: "an education method or philosophy where learners choose their activities rather than being directed." I don't particularly like either definition of the word "unschooling" to be related to homeschooling. The first one gives the impression of not educating our children at all. And with the second definition of unschooling, students are NOT going to know enough about topics to choose those things that need to be learned.

I preferred to allow my children to "rabbit" off into interests from topics we presented for them to learn. I encouraged "Why?" "When?" "Where?" and "How?" questions that led to deeper learning experiences. We provided books, field trips, and other resources to enhance their learning, even into high school. We called it "rabbiting" because our last name is Abbitt, and I just thought that we would rabbit (not squirrel) off to learn more related things. My children got a good education; we just didn't do school the "normal" way. In my opinion, guided, "Non-Traditional", experiential learning is a better way to describe how we homeschooled. We still used some books and workbooks, but we enhanced them with projects, field trips and more.

In the 1990s, when events started being put on by homeschoolers for homeschoolers, colleges and universities began to pay to have booths at these events to recruit homeschooled high school students to their colleges. I had a college admissions advisor say that she could acclimate a homeschool student to college easier than a traditional school student. She went on to explain that due to all the promptings to go to class, to turn in homework, and to behave that students receive in traditional schools, students expect this help at college, and this is not going to happen for them at college. She said they will either figure it out or go home. She went on to say that homeschoolers seem to know how to show up for class, do their homework, and don't tend to get drunk and destroy the campus.

Since the early days of homeschooling, it has been documented that home educated students typically scored as well or higher on standardized testing than traditional school students. Could it be that the love for learning, one-on-one tutoring, or remediating to mastery have made the difference? Could it be that the people who care most about their child's education are the ones in charge of that education?   A home-educated student who is allowed to learn to their fullest potential can be successful in whatever their pursuits are, whether it be getting a college education, pursuing a career, or as parents who homeschool the next generation.

Myth 62: *My child must go to college in order to get a good job.*

TRUTH: There are many ways to get a good job and be successful with and without a college degree.

One of our children started college and was doing very well but realized that even if he spent his time getting a college degree, he would still have to get certifications in order to pursue the career he was interested in. After one semester of college, he got a job working for a company that would pay for the first certifications he needed. Then he was able to get a better job that would pay for higher certifications in his field.   Then he was offered the opportunity to have the most expensive certification paid for if he would work for 4 years. With this certification he became a journeyman welder with no college debt and was able to earn money along the way.

There are a lot of great jobs today that pay very well and that do not require a college education. Skilled labor is in big demand as a huge majority of the skilled labor force are getting old enough to retire. Society has spent decades pushing for a college degree instead of hands-on careers. Where there is a need or demand, you will find higher paying jobs. Many people thrive in more experiential occupations and are perfect for trade jobs even if they struggled to read and write by school standards. As my friend would say, "God created men to be builders and most men enjoy work that allows them to build, make, and do something that makes a difference." There are additional ways people have found to have a good income without a college degree:

- side hustles – work performed to supplement the income of your primary job;
- multiples streams of income – making money from more than one source helps achieve goals and objectives;
- entrepreneurship - allows for using skills to start a new business;
- passive income – comes from something that already exists that one is not actively working to receive.

You can begin encouraging your students to look for opportunities for them to pursue their talents, interests, and jobs while in high school. If these experiences don't become their career, these skills may be used throughout life in other ways.

Remember: Whether you choose a college degree, trade school, or one of the other additional job opportunities, you are only limited by your work ethic, willingness to learn, and your imagination. The sky is the limit!

Myth 63: *I can't teach critical thinking skills.*

TRUTH: Critical thinking skills are learned best in normal life experiences. Life is full of problems to solve; allow your student to experience life, work a job, and help with the family and home.

Critical thinking is the key to building problem solving skills. In traditional education, students are taught to read the books that are given to them and regurgitate the information onto a test. This has left us with many in society who need someone to tell them what to think. Many will blindly go where they are told to go and fear what they are told to fear.

Home-educated students can learn a lot of problem solving skills through real-world experiences if we, as parents, don't automatically give our children the answers. Instead, we should ask questions like what they think could be done about any particular situation and then give them time to think and respond. Sometimes they come up with ideas and solutions that are better than what we could have thought of. When you see your children's eyes light up with understanding you know critical thinking is taking place.

Critical thinking can be naturally learned through experiences of life, work, and home. The most important outcome of being a critical thinker is that your student will ask 'why' questions. They will learn to ask great questions and not blindly believe everything that someone tells them. Instead, if they use critical thinking, they will rationally examine the truth and determine if it makes sense to believe or act on what they have been told.

Remember: You CAN raise your child in the way they should go and end up with an ADULT who will know HOW to think and be prepared for their life ahead.

CONCLUSION

As we come to the conclusion of this book, there are so many more stories to tell and words of encouragement to offer. But as I conclude this book there are a few nuggets of **TRUTH** I want you to **REMEMBER**.

During the journey educating my children, my goal was not to raise kids. But rather, I wanted independent, critical-thinking adults. When I got to the end of the journey with my children, I looked back to see what really mattered most to help my children be equipped to be successful adults. This is what I realized they needed the most. They needed to:

- **Love to Learn** "If you teach your children to love to learn, they will learn for the rest of their lives."
- **Know how they learn best**. "You will never teach your child everything, but if they know how to learn, they will never stop learning."
- **Have a good Work Ethic**. You can be the smartest person at college or a job, but if you don't show up and do the work required, you won't last long.
- **Be Problem Solvers:** People can keep a better attitude if they don't feel stuck, but rather know how to look for solutions.
- **Look to God** for the answers because He is the One your children will need to direct them through their lives when you are not there.

Imagine if, from the beginning, education actually allowed children to explore their world and identify their strengths and talents instead of letting them all follow the same pattern of education and leaving them frustrated in life after graduation. **That is what we get to do, folks.** We get to allow our children to explore and identify their strengths and their talents and figure out what God created them to be. You can feel confident that they don't have to fit in a box. **AND** they don't have to be like everybody else! It's freeing to realize that it's okay to be different; God made each of us for different purposes. As we accept that we are each different then we can appreciate other people being different from us. We can drop the chains, open the cage, and be set free to educate in the way that is best for our families. Embrace the flexibility and freedom to educate your children as uniquely as God created them to be. Knowing these **TRUTHS**, I believe, will set you free to teach your children the way they learn best.

You've got a lot of options. So, if something's not working for your child... **STOP, PRAY, and CHANGE** to something else until you find what works. If you need additional help, you can reach out to me. I love to help parents figure out what works best for them and their children. It is my hope that the **TRUTHS** shared have cut through the chains of any **MYTHS** that may have kept you caged. As you consider the best educational path for you and your children, know that you are not alone on this journey, and that you, like me and so many others, can be **Set Free to Homeschool**.

CUT THE CHAINS OF TRADITIONAL
SCHOOL THINKING

BE SET FREE TO HOMESCHOOL
THE WAY THAT IT WORKS BEST
FOR YOUR STUDENT

RESOURCES

The amount resources available today are overwhelming; so here are links to a few that I have had experience with and have found these to be very helpful.

For more options and information
PLEASE CHECK OUT:

Set Free to Homeschool YouTube Channel

http://www.youtube.com/@SetFreetoHomeschool

WEBSITE
The Home School Counseling Team

https://homeschoolcounselingteam.com/

WORKSHOPS IDEAS FOR EVENT SPEAKING:

Set Free to Homeschool: It's Not Traditional School

Set Free to Survive High School and enjoy the Journey aka Don't Stress Out Over High School

How To Survive Homeschooling (Practical Tips)

How Children Learn Best

Set Free from Guilt (Homeschooling without Guilt)

Homeschool 101 - How to Get Started

Set Free to Homeschool a Large Family

Set Free to Work Together and How to Make It Work

How to set up co-ops using a unit study approach to learning

Please email setfreetohomeschool@gmail.com about Margie speaking at your upcoming event or conference.

Other Resources:

Biblioplan

www.biblioplan.net

Exploration Education Physical Education

https://explorationeducation.com/year-long-physical-science/#

Homeschooling with Dyslexia

https://homeschoolingwithdyslexia.com/

Inspiring Minds

www.inspiringmindslearningcenter.com

KONOS

www.konos.com

KONOS History of the World

https://konos.com/high-school/?v=7516fd43adaa

Movies as Literature

https://www.designastudy.com

Natural Speller

www.designastudy.com/language-arts/natural-speller/

NOTGRASS History

www.notgrass.com

Parents That Fight

www.parentswhofight.com

The 101 Series Science Series:

www.the101series.com

The Mystery of History

www.themysteryofhistory.com

Triad Math

www.homeschoolmathcrusade.com/

Triad Tribe

https://triadmathinc.com/family/

Triad Tribe is a membership that provides your family with Triad Math,
The Home School Counseling Team,
and Wisdom Webinars.

Checkout Curriculum Reviews by
This Homeschooling Adventure
for

Movies As Literature

https://www.youtube.com/watch?v=awJGizoWyq8

Biology 101

https://www.youtube.com/watch?v=AsUPOFvXCsg&t=82s

Chemistry 101

https://www.youtube.com/watch?v=jk2k89NhLFY

Physics 101

https://www.youtube.com/watch?v=QlBF3DCRntY

ABOUT THE AUTHOR

Margie Abbitt has been married to her best friend, Mac, for over 40 years. They homeschooled their "Brady Bunch" of 3 boys and 3 girls. Margie homeschooled in NC, PA, OH, IN, MI and then TN using a variety of curriculum and teaching methods to meet the needs of many diversified students. She especially enjoys a unit study / hands-on approach to teaching, because learning should be fun and active. Margie has organized, led, and taught in co-ops/tutorials for over 25 years. Margie has had the privilege of working with families and students from many varied backgrounds, learning styles and challenges as an academic counselor. She has a passion for helping parents/grandparents navigate their homeschool experience while encouraging them in their homeschooling journey.

www.ingramcontent.com/pod-product-compliance
Lightning Source LLC
LaVergne TN
LVHW051232080426
835513LV00016B/1545